HISTORY
AND
HISTORICAL
UNDERSTANDING

edited by
C. T. McIntire and Ronald A. Wells

GRAND RAPIDS, MICHIGAN
WILLIAM B. EERDMANS PUBLISHING COMPANY

Copyright ©1984 by William B. Eerdmans Publishing Co.
255 Jefferson Ave. SE, Grand Rapids, Mich. 49503

Library of Congress Cataloging in Publication Data
Main entry under title:

History and historical understanding.

Includes index.
Contents: Scripture, history, and the quest for meaning
/ Langdon Gilkey—Historical study and the historical
dimension of our world / C. T. McIntire—The difference
in being a Christian and the difference it makes—for
history / Martin E. Marty—[etc.]
1. History (Theology)—Addresses, essays, lectures.
2. Historiography—Addresses, essays, lectures.
I. McIntire, C. T. II. Wells, Ronald, 1941–   .
BR115.H5H53   1984   231.7′6   84-13804

ISBN 0-8028-0030-0

Contents

Preface   vii
Contributors   xi

1. LANGDON GILKEY   **Scripture, History, and the Quest for Meaning**   3

2. C. T. MCINTIRE   **Historical Study and the Historical Dimension of Our World**   17

3. MARTIN E. MARTY   **The Difference in Being a Christian and the Difference it Makes—for History**   41

4. GEORGE MARSDEN   **Common Sense and the Spiritual Vision of History**   55

5. M. HOWARD RIENSTRA   **History, Objectivity, and the Christian Scholar**   69

6. ROBERT T. HANDY   **Christian Faith and Historical Method: Contradiction, Compromise, or Tension?**   83

7. ROBERT P. SWIERENGA   **Social Science History: An Appreciative Critique**   93

8. DALE VAN KLEY   **Christianity, Christian Interpretation, and the Origins of the French Revolution**   103

Notes   125
Index   143

Preface

THIS BOOK is presented in the belief that the historical task is ongoing. Historians using modern critical methods and assumptions must eschew triumphalism and didacticism at every turn. We stand in a tradition of conversation about history, and it is no more than the truth for us to say that we would like these essays to take their place in that ongoing task. Some nine years ago, the William B. Eerdmans Publishing Company brought out a set of essays edited by George M. Marsden and Frank Roberts entitled *A Christian View of History?* While the essays in this book would not necessarily pretend to supersede those of 1975, we would suggest that they represent another step in the development of the conversation. In fact, three of the essayists in the Marsden/ Roberts volume have also written essays for this book. It is with a combination of humility and excitement that we offer these new essays for scholars and students alike.

The twentieth century has been an unnerving one for historians. If we accept with E. H. Carr that history is a dialogue between present and past, the present from which we reflect on the past fills us with disquietude. The main difference between our perception of the relationship between present and past and that of earlier historians is that we have lost that most elementary, yet crucial, support of their historiography—the view of history as progress. Moreover, we have no broad agreement on any comparable or more adequate view of history to put in its place. It would seem that the events of our century warrant belief not in progress but in the possibility of endless crisis.

If there has been, at least since Barth, a theology of crisis, there may also be a historiography of crisis. This has set many people wondering about the course of history. What are the historiographical consequences of admitting, with Robert Heilbroner, that "the outlook for man . . . is painful, difficult, perhaps desperate, and the hope that can be held out for his future prospect seems to be very slim indeed" (*An Inquiry Into the Human Prospect,* 22)? For Christians, these consequences are of great moment. Christians have always been among those thinking about history, and they have produced a lively tradition of Christian reflection on history—in which this volume would take its place.

We certainly are prompted by, and have in view, the large questions of the crises of our civilization; but we find it worthwhile to get at them, not directly, but by a circuitous route into another realm of discourse to gather resources for understanding historical concerns. What we present is a consideration of some questions in which religion, philosophy, and history interact, because these three disciplines share the task of historical understanding. Here we approach our interdisciplinary concern from the angle of history.

The common theme of these essays is the attempt to get at what insights Christian faith may bring to our understanding of historical process and historical knowledge and study, and then the exploration of what we may gain from such insights. The special quality of our attempt is that we very consciously refuse to limit our discussion to what may be called "theology of history"—about God, providence, Christ in history, salvation in history, and the meaning of history. Instead, we wish to work the other way around, to begin our analysis with the everyday reality of ordinary history—the history we live and the history that historians write about. We use Christian religious language and insights, but we claim that what we have to say is not simply about theology but about historical process and historical study. Our claim is enhanced by the fact that eight of the nine contributors to this volume are historians. We have learned what we know about history in many ways, including our experience in current history and our professional pursuit of teaching, researching, and writing history. Our teaching and writings are about many varieties of history—social, economic, political, diplomatic, intellectual, ecclesiastical. Moreover, against the potential objection that these essays remain too much on the level of abstract thinking, we refer readers to our other writings. The partial list of our writings on the contributors' page will give readers some indication of the kinds of "case studies" we believe to be important in conjunction with the more theoretical work done here.

Our essays represent attempts to regather our thoughts as Christians in this secular age of crisis. The days are gone when a Christian interpretation of history meant mainly talking about God in history, looking for God's action and judgment or the advance of his purposes in, say, the defeat of the Spanish Armada, or the famine that cut the population of mid-nineteenth-century Ireland in half, or the prosperity of the American nation. The Old Testament is no longer a model for writing history, as it was for hundreds of years. Instead, we are affirming that history and historical study properly have to do with people along with the nonhuman world, and that we may beneficially pursue the study and understanding of human and nonhuman history with the aid of Christian faith and insight. Not all the contributors to this volume agree with each other, and no one of us holds anyone else responsible for what he expresses. We do agree, however, that Christian faith should not be peripheral, or additional, to academic learning, but that faith may be an integrative power intrinsic to historical analysis.

There is a thematic flow to the essays. We begin with Langdon Gilkey's suggestion of the great complexity of the historical process. In the quest for meaning, in modern cultures and indeed in all cultures, scriptures seem to be a universal imperative. If there is hope in the midst of crisis, the nature of the hope turns on the recognition that "transcendence has creatively entered the scene and made all the difference." Gilkey sees the Christian Bible as the beginning point of that recognition. C. T. McIntire offers some suggestions about the structure of the historical process. With a specific focus on time and culture-making, he suggests that history can be seen as a discipline with integrative traits. Martin Marty directly asks the question implicit in all the essays: What difference does being a Christian make in the actual doing of history? And George Marsden also takes up that theme in the essay that follows. Both writers suggest that while Christian claims for the intrusion of the transcendent in history cannot be verified by the canons of analytical historical scholarship, the Christian vocation of history nevertheless offers certain unique angles of vision that can illumine historical reality. M. Howard Rienstra's essay continues that theme by looking at "objectivity" in recent historical thought, most notably in relationship to "control beliefs." On the matter of objectivity, Robert T. Handy identifies a tension between Christian faith and historical method; but he suggests creative uses to which that tension can be put in the writing of narrative history. Robert Swierenga discusses the merits and demerits of the "new social science" history; this wide-ranging essay indicates how social science methods may relate to other historical methods. Finally, Dale K. Van Kley investigates one of the most complex and hotly debated specific historical problems—the origins of the French revolution—in an essay that shows how a balanced and Christian view of human nature may help overcome the difficulties of other, more one-dimensional approaches. The integrality of these essays, then, can be stated in technical terms: the essays treat, in order, historical ontology, epistemology, method, and interpretation of events.

All the essays began as papers or lectures and have been revised for publication in this volume. Four essays were originally presented at a conference in Chicago on the theme of the philosophy of history, which was sponsored by the Conference on Faith and History, an affiliate of the American Historical Association. Marty and Handy originally presented their essays at the Institute for Christian Studies in Toronto, and Van Kley presented his to a conference of Christian teachers at Calvin College.

Our hope is that these essays will contribute to a better understanding of history and historical study, and that in this way we may gain a few more resources for understanding the crises of our age and for taking such action ourselves as contributes to the health of our world.

C. T. McINTIRE
Toronto

RONALD A. WELLS
Grand Rapids

Pentecost, 1984

Contributors

LANGDON GILKEY (Ph.D., Columbia) is Shailer Matthews Professor of Theology at The Divinity School of The University of Chicago, and past president of the American Academy of Religion. Notable among his books is *Reaping the Whirlwind: A Christian Interpretation of History* (Seabury, 1977).

ROBERT T. HANDY (Ph.D., Chicago) is author of *A History of the Churches in the United States and Canada* (Oxford, 1977) and *Christian America: Protestant Hopes and Historical Realities* (Oxford, 1971, 1983). He is Professor of Church History and former Dean at Union Theological Seminary in New York City.

GEORGE MARSDEN (Ph.D., Yale) published *The Evangelical Mind and the New School Presbyterian Experience* (Yale, 1970), *Fundamentalism and American Culture* (Oxford, 1980), and coedited *A Christian View of History?* (Eerdmans, 1975). He is Professor of History at Calvin College.

MARTIN E. MARTY (Ph.D., Chicago) is Fairfax M. Cone Distinguished Service Professor of the History of Modern Christianity at The University of Chicago, an editor of *Church History,* and past president of both the American Society of Church History and the American Catholic Historical Association. He is author of *Righteous Empire: The Protestant Experience in America* (Harper and Row, 1970), *A Nation of Behavers* (Chicago, 1976), and many other books.

C. T. MCINTIRE (Ph.D., Pennsylvania) is Associate Professor of History at Trinity College in the University of Toronto, author of *England against the Papacy, 1858-1861* (Cambridge, 1983), and editor of *God, History, and Historians* (Oxford, 1977) and *Herbert Butterfield: Writings on Christianity and History* (Oxford, 1979). Previously he taught at the Institute for Christian Studies, Toronto.

M. HOWARD RIENSTRA (Ph.D., Michigan) is Professor of History at Calvin College and has written numerous articles and essays on historiography, bibliography, and Italian history.

ROBERT P. SWIERENGA (Ph.D., Iowa), Professor of History at Kent State University, edited *Quantification in American History: Theory and Research* (Atheneum, 1970) and wrote *Pioneers and Profits: Land Speculation on the Iowa Frontier* (Iowa State, 1968) as well as many articles on quantification and immigrant history. He is an editor of the journal *Social Science History.*

DALE VAN KLEY (Ph.D., Yale) wrote *The Jansenists and the Expulsion of the Jesuits from France, 1757–1765* (Yale, 1975) and *To Kill a King: the Damiens Affair and the Unravelling of the Old Regime in France, 1750–1770* (Princeton, 1983). He is Professor of History at Calvin College.

RONALD A. WELLS (Ph.D., Boston) has published *Conflict and Christianity in Northern Ireland* (Eerdmans, 1975) and edited *The Wars of America* (Eerdmans, 1981) and *Letters of a Young Immigrant in Manitoba* (University of Manitoba, 1981). He is Professor of History at Calvin College and past editor of the journal *Fides et Historia.*

HISTORY
AND
HISTORICAL
UNDERSTANDING

1. Scripture, History, and the Quest for Meaning

LANGDON GILKEY

OUR THEME is the relationship of Scripture and its understanding to the understanding of history, to the discernment of meaning or the promise of meaning in history's sequences. This relationship has been taken for granted in the long tradition of Hebrew and Christian thought about history and its meaning. For us, it is here in the biblical volume that there is contained the light that illumines the dark, terrifying mystery of historical existence and that offers promise not only of understanding but of creative courage and hope. And yet we must recognize that this correlation of Scripture and history seems anachronistic, parochial, and bizarre to the world around us, a kind of methodological version, so to say, of Lessing's "ugly ditch." If it be absurd to derive a truth of universal scope from one historical event, surely it is equally backward to interpret universal history on the basis of one text—and one text which represents a variety of epochs and cultural situations and is crammed with diverse materials and wildly divergent viewpoints at that.

Clearly, as Barth would say, this queer claim to manifest the universal can become intelligible only through the category of revelation: only the divine Word can leap the "ugly ditch" from the particular to the universal; only through the Word can one text bear this transcendent role in truth and in grace. Granting that point to Barth, however—and speaking as a systematic theologian, I agree thoroughly with him on it—I think it true, nonetheless, that this correlation of one text, especially a religious text, with the interpretation and comprehension of history is not as bizarre and naive as modern culture tends to see it. To most of the modern consciousness, liberal or Marxist, history is not at all an impenetrable mystery. On the contrary, all one has to do is "look at it" carefully and responsibly, "empirically and scientifically" as we would say, to see its structure and so to understand the principles of its sequences and changes. In such an endeavor, how can one text or one tradition be given a crucial role? And in such an obviously *secular* endeavor, comprised at best of economic, political, psychological, and historical learning, insight, and methodologies, how can a *religious* text be relevant or helpful, let alone decisive? It is this viewpoint that I wish here to contest as a misunderstanding of the way

3

we, as humans, are in history and the way, consequently, we understand history and find meaning in it.

Texts, religious symbols, and participatory principles of interpretation dominate and shape every approach to history and to life within it; this is a pattern pervasive in cultural and communal interpretations of history. And not only that, I shall seek to suggest that an understanding of history based on Scripture fits the contours of history as we experience it. This dual argument does not constitute a natural theology. Only in the brightest and happiest of epochs, and then only among the privileged classes, is a natural theology based on the character of *history* conceivable. Thus, our argument presupposes some transcendent principle of meaning, that is to say, it presupposes revelation which no natural theology can establish or encompass. Nevertheless, it is an apologetical argument based on the compatibility or correlation of history as experienced and comprehended with history as interpreted in Scripture—a correlation basic, I believe, to Scripture's own understanding of itself and its historical world.

The Structure of History and the Need for Scriptures

Let us begin this discussion with what will seem obvious about human being in time as we experience it. Humans, it has often been said, are both in and out of history, immersed in it and yet transcending it. Thus arise the two senses of the word *history:* as the sequence itself of novel and unpredictable events and as a report on or interpretation of that sequence. For it is evident that human existence is in and out of history in two related but distinct ways. First of all, our being in history is characterized by the polarity of destiny and freedom: of a given (destiny) from our own past and that of our world which constitutes us, forms and shapes us, pushes us inexorably in a given, determined direction, and with which—whether we will or no—we must deal in all our actions. This unremovable destiny is balanced by the unavoidable requirement to decide and to act now in creative response to that given, within its limits but in the light of its possibilities (freedom). Thus is history characterized by trends and continuities arising out of a given destiny, and by contingency and novelty arising out of the unpredictability of human responses, decisions, and actions in the face of that given. The given was once itself undetermined, itself mere possibility; now it is there, shaped, unavoidable. What we do with it is limited by these conditions but never determined by them; conditions, said Gordon Leff, become history only when they elicit a human response. History is destiny in union with freedom, neither one alone. We are "in" history as we are dependent on the conditions given from beyond ourselves; we are "out" of it as we are capable or responding in novel ways to those conditions. In history, actuality is balanced by possibility and destiny by freedom; and the union of the two makes historical events.

Second, while we are *in* the stream of history, pushed by it in unwanted directions, threatened by its plethora of menacing forces, and lured by its unexpected possibilities, humans are also "out of it" in memory and anticipation. Spirit transcends history by surveying its past and in that light envisioning its possible future, by uniting, in other words, its destiny and its freedom, its unavoidable actualities from the past and its range of possibilities for the future. In each act of freedom in relation to destiny—in each personal and each political act—remembered past and anticipated future are brought together first in comprehension and then in decision. Again, embeddedness in time and transcendence of it unite to make event. Thus does eternity, transcending time but a transcendence united with time, invade personal and communal life in historical understanding and in political actions alike.

In any case, it is for this ontological reason—because of the character or structure of human being in time—that it is necessary, for any historical understanding to be achieved or for any personal or political act to take place, to bring what is remembered and interpreted and what is perhaps to come into a meaningful unity, a unity of understanding and of meaning, so that ongoing life, creative action toward the future, is possible. The deep involvement of human being and meaning *in* historical passage, *in* history, and yet its ability to survey and partially to direct that passage, together make it necessary to give to the sequences of time a logos, a structure of order and meaning within which both understanding and purposive action become possible. Political consciousness is requisite for political action, and a *theory* about the sequence of events is necessary for both.

Political action is both unavoidable and central in historical existence. It represents the action of a centered community, through its "legitimate" leaders, in response to the given crises and opportunities of its common life. Since we all exist communally, political action is thus the way freedom expresses itself and is present in community, that is, in historical life. And for a political act expressive of freedom, as for historical reflection itself, a unified understanding of the past and present, and thus of the possibilities of our future, is necessary. Also involved or presupposed in creative action is a firm grasp of the norms and the potential meanings of life in time. In history and so in communal life, the practical and the theoretical tend to fuse into one— as the continuous role of savants or wise men in active political life illustrates. And both presuppose a vision of the structure and the meaning of the total sequence of events in which that community finds itself.

For these reasons, deeply embedded in our ontological structure as "finite freedom"—as *in* yet *out of* history—myths, the symbolic visions of history as a whole, appear as basic to all important political speech; and a general vision of history is presupposed in all historical understanding, even that which claims to be "scientific." Ingredient in these myths or visions of history—at least as they function communally—is some understanding of the ultimate sovereignty that rules history and its magisterial or ruling forces, be they evolutionary, economic, psychological, or theological; some view of an ultimate order in these sequences; some vision of an ultimate norm for communal life in history; and some sense for its ultimate meaning and hence for grounds for a shared hope. Classically organized "religions" have provided the symbolic structure that orients communal life in time to some permanent order and meaning. In a secular world, so-called ideologies, for example, liberal progressivism and Marxism, have done the same thing. Thus are politics and religion deeply intertwined in communal life. For it is the mythical vision (religious or secular) structuring this order and meaning of history that provides the basis for legitimate political rule, the guidelines for acceptable political action, the standards and goals for society's vocations, and the aims for its patterns of education. Every culture, as Tillich reminded us, has such a "religious substance" and apprehension of ultimate being that structures our ultimate concerns, and that, as we have indicated, symbolically structures the ultimate and sacred horizon within which each community and each facet of its culture lives and becomes in time.

No wonder, then, that history, politics, and religion have always been so deeply intertwined. It is within the ongoing stream of historical process that communities face the crucial issues of their life and death, of security and insecurity, of freedom from fate or subservience to it, of the enhancement or loss of meaningful existence—that is to say, "religious" issues. And it is here in the sequences of temporal change that their freedom is most sorely tempted to actions of vast sin or self-destruction, or that they are called on for strength, courage, justice, and compassion. The issues of our being and of our nonbeing, our ultimate concerns, appear as much for communal life as for individual existence *within* historical sequence, in dealing with an unavoidable given and in facing an unknown and often uncontrollable future.

Despite all their knowledge and technology, modern men and women have not transcended this ontological structure of temporality and finitude, not escaped the terrors and anxieties of history, the threats of fate and of nonbeing menacing their future, nor lost their need for confidence and hope in the open possibilities for that future. Thus is there a religious dimension in all cultural life and to all political speech and understanding, as much in contemporary as in ancient times. As a consequence, theological understanding—the understanding of the meaning of historical being in terms of religious-type symbols—is always relevant to the comprehension of history. Or, to put it another way, any global understanding of history—again one thinks of liberalism or Marxism—foundational for political and theoretical life alike, has a religious or a theological dimension or component. It includes a mythical structure providing to those who are committed to it an understanding of their own role in the global history of good or evil, an ultimate norm for cultural life, and a sense of meaning and of hope for the unknown future. To correlate *religious* documents structured by *religious* symbols with the interpretation of history is, therefore, by no means aberrant or merely traditional. Each modern secular ideology straining to be based on science or historical understanding alone takes to itself religious elements whenever it functions as the common schema for the interpretation of a community's vital history.

Despite their necessity, such global visions of history are hard to come by and harder to verify. As every culture (except perhaps our own) has realized, the order and meaning of the structure of historical events is at best opaque, its key elusive: it represents a mystery with only dim and fragmentary facets of meaning. And it is certainly true that history presents us with an exceedingly complex and rich scene. As the story of collective human action in relation to natural changes, it includes all the multifaceted dimensions, factors, and "causes" characteristic of indivdual human existence. To seek to understand it as if it were merely an aspect of nature characterized by invariant and determined physical relations alone, by "social laws," is thus a serious methodological error. Contingency and freedom are deeply ingredient in its structure, and so the possibility of real alternatives and the actuality of unexpected novelty continually upset any simple causal or rational order.

Three other factors add to this complexity and opaqueness of history:

1) Curious observers of history, however objective they may seek to be, are themselves involved in the history they observe, ultimately concerned with the direction of its current—for their life itself slides on it or sinks because of it. Thus are their visions shaped by their interests, and their interests by their location in the historical order. The fortunes or misfortunes of their class, sex, race, nation, epoch give form to their views and shape the optimistic mood that governs every such vision. For this reason, myths about history, unless subjected radically to critique, are both partial and ideological: each is a limited

perspective directed all too sharply by special interest as well as particular insight.

2) The sequences of history that are surveyed are always incomplete. Thus the significance of each event, like election returns early on, is not yet "in" and so the meaning—even of a short span of events—is as yet neither settled nor evident. Consequently, visions of history are at best studied guesses, projected hypotheses, matters as much of communal commitment and hope as of any precise verification or clear conceptual understanding. They are in fact "religious myths," held communally for existential as well as theoretical reasons, massively influencing life but limited in their universality and verifiability.

Any tomorrow can effect radical changes in the meaning of every piece of the data on which a vision of history is built. In a brief span of time a novel sequence of important events can sink the most formidable and apparently permanent social or economic trend almost without a trace. Two examples come immediately to mind: predictions of a stable future made in the Richmond, Virginia or Montgomery, Alabama of 1856 would have seemed bizarre indeed in 1875. And even Herman Kahn, who boasted that a scientific futurology would at last peer reliably into our probable future, had in his 1970 book on the future as yet no intimations at all of the ecology crisis, the crisis of world natural resources, that was to explode and only two years later qualify every expectation about our common world future. The past is itself not yet finished, and the future is radically unknown and unknowable. These ontological facts both elicit our need for a meaningful vision for this opaque passage in which we are, and yet they too prevent us from being clear about what we dimly see or very certain about the validity of our reports and our vision of things to come.

3) History is alienated or estranged from its own structure. It seems never to be what it could or should be, what its possibilities either promise or require. Since this alienation arises in large part from our freedom, it includes our common responsibility. History, said Tillich, is estranged, and its estrangement is sin; or, as Augustine and Niebuhr said, history is "fallen," and we are each alone and altogether involved in that fall. As theory, this sounds bizarre, moralistic, and even "small town" or naive. As experience, however, it is continually validated. Glowing possibilities, both personal and social, do sour and become tasteless or demonic. Think of the waxing power of Europe in the seventeenth and eighteenth centuries, or that of America in the postwar world. And yet now the power of Europe is gone, and that of America declining—and each is for the foreseeable future paying dearly for the exploitation, the oppression, and the conflicts that characterized the ways each actualized its own possiblities. The "given" that each older

generation presents to its children—what they have done with their world, so full of possibilities in their youth—festers as they hand it on with hidden or open sores that cause endless pain and can become lethal for the new generation that follows. My father's generation inherited from its parents the effects of World War I; mine, Hitler's world and World War II; and think what a mass of tangled corruption, of a world fraught with demonic possibilities, our children will inherit from us. This corruption of history's ideal possibilities is the experienced actuality of history. This actuality, to be sure, is clearer in some ages and to some groups than it is to others; but it is characteristic of all times and places. Yet it is also true that in the midst of this deep alienation characteristic of actuality, possibilities of the creative new do still appear, hope and confidence are deeply felt, and unexpected healing is experienced.

Thus is there added to the complexity of history, and the involvement of every observer in it, a further dialectical complexity that requires a very subtle and rich—and also "religious"—set of categories. First, there is the ontological-anthropological structure of the history of destiny and freedom whereby each finite actuality is or can be given new possibilities for the future. Second, there is the experienced alienation whereby destiny becomes fate, and freedom seems stripped of genuine possibilities. And finally—a "fact" expressed in all religious visions—there appear redemptive forces of healing, reconciliation, reunion, and new beginnings. For this reason, secular theories of history become ideologies when they begin to function socially: that is, they all finally include a depiction of the career of good in the midst of evil, a story of redemption, however unintelligible or unempirical it may be, from the evil that obscures our historical present. And thus are recognized religious visions of history often more subtle and therefore more empirical (that is, closer to the facts of history) than are most purely cognitive scientific or philosophical visions. For each religious view tends to include some version of this religious dialectic established by alienation and redemption, as well as the ontological limits and possibilities inherent in finitude and in freedom. No general interpretation of history can ignore the pervasive patterns of evil that engulf historical life, any more than it can ignore the possibilities implicit in freedom. Without a religious dialectic of alienation and redemption, however, such views *mis*interpret those patterns evident in historical life, either emphasizing the positive structure and hence the possibilities of historical life (if the observer belongs to a fortunate group in a fortunate epoch) in an unwarranted and soon-to-be falsified optimism, or concentrating so heavily on the actuality of evil that they fail to discern the new possibilities and the forces for reconciliation latent in historical experience.

Biblical symbolism includes each of these levels of dialectical complexity, and that is perhaps the explanation for whatever persuasive theoretical power it may possess. In its symbols of creation and providence and its consequent understanding of human existence as dependent finitude, and yet free and directed to the ultimate and the sacred, that is, as creaturely and yet made in the image of God, it presents a structural or ontological understanding of existence that clarifies and affirms the finitude and yet the self-transcendence characteristic of human life in time. With its further "religious" categories of estrangement and sin on the one hand, and of revelation, redemption, and reconciliation on the other, it encompasses the second dialectic pervasive in existence we have just outlined.

It should be noted, however, that this illuminating complexity has led to two divergent and often clashing interpretations of biblical symbolism. Seen from the perspective of this dialectical complexity, both of these antithetical traditions take their rightful place as legitimate on the one hand but as partial on the other. One of them, conceived usually in an optimistic era, and from a privileged spot in which personal and historical possibilities seem plentiful, sees clearly the fundamental ontological structure of creative destiny and of pervasive freedom for new possibilities. Thus discerning an order and meaning to history's sequences, it concludes "rationally" that this evident goodness of life requires and hence implies a divine power, a divine wisdom, and a divine bounty. When the ontological structure of history can be clearly seen, natural theologies and philosophical theisms abound and dominate theological reflection; but understandably such theologies, based on an apprehension of the obvious goodness and meaning of ordinary life, can only dimly discern the tragic elements of existence and so barely appreciate the full scope and meaning of the gospel.

In contrast, for other biographies and epochs, the alienation, the fatedness, and the suffering of history are deeply experienced. Destiny, with its promise, has consistently become a closed fatedness to suffering and to meaninglessness, and the hope for new possibilities seems only an illusion. Freedom is aware only of its own bondage and its responsibility for that bondage. Sin, fate, and death appear alone to be the factors that rule actuality. In that sort of situation, the ontological structure of history as characterized by freedom and possibility disappears as do landmarks in a deep fog at sea. And at that point, suave clerical assurances of the goodness, order, and possibilities of life seem to be cruel jests if they are not ideological shams, a turning away from obvious injustice in order to maintain exploitative privilege. The longing for rescue from the anxiety, terror, and guilt of historical actuality replaces grateful celebration of its maker and serene confidence in divine justice. Understandably now, the more "religious" and less philosophical categories of sin and grace come to the fore as characterizing experienced actuality. Creation and providence, although still providing the ontological grounds for God's judgment and God's grace alike, seem ideologically suspect, a self-interested justification and blessing of an evil world. Here too, however, a theological error can appear if this emphasis is pushed too far. For the gospel and the promises of grace make no sense unless the world is God's creation and under God's ultimate sovereignty. Both of these interpretations are, therefore, genuine intuitions of the character of historical existence, and both emphasize essential and thus crucial biblical symbols—and each consistently detests the vision of history and of the Christian religion that the other proffers! Possibly, an awareness of the complexity and the opaqueness, even the mystery and depth, of historical process will help us appreciate the dialectical richness and even the apparent paradoxes of our common biblical symbolism.

In any case, the main thrust of our argument is that both the character of human participation in history and the consequent complexity of history call for mythical and theological understanding. We cannot just "look at" history to uncover either the structure or the meaning of its sequences. Some deep assumed principle of interpretation is always at work whenever we think about temporal passage or seek to act within it. Such presupposed principles answer questions about the relationship of determinism and freedom, about the meaning and scope of evil in time, about the possibilities available to life in time, about the redemptive forces available or not in history—in short, a global or mythical vision compounded of philosophical, psychological, and religious elements.

The history of religions provides us with explicitly religious variants of these global symbol systems; modern ideologies such as liberalism and Marxism provide us with secular versions of the same. Each shapes and gives substance to a community's life by uniting that community through its vision of history and the role it gives that community in history. The religious substance of each creative culture is largely constituted by a vision of history and of its meaning. Each is in turn quite particular; each arises out of a religious or cultural tradition; each had crucial tests to which to appeal. Thus not only religious symbols but also participation in a tradition, and attention if not adherence to the texts formative of that tradition, are constitutive elements of any communal interpretation of history. The logos of history is in each case born by a given tradition and embodied in a given set of "scriptures," and both are crucial for communal and political existence. History and interpretation, history and texts, are correlative. For historical beings, the universal is only available *through* the particularity of a given tradition and its texts, the meaning of history through a particular cultural or religious viewpoint. The role of Scripture or its equivalent in human life in history, in shaping and unifying community, in guiding action, and in comprehending the future with courage and hope, is no Christian or Jewish aberration destined to die out. It is essential to our human historicity.

The Biblical Scriptures and History

Having discussed and defended the particular—in tradition, symbolic structure, and scriptural texts—as essential to the interpretation of past history and to action within present and future history, I will now turn directly to our particular case, to our scriptures, and see how they serve to discern the meaning of events as we experience the latter. Do they illuminate the structure and meaning of historical passage? and does this illumination provide a creative framework, inspiration, and guide for praxis? I think they do—though any arguments at this level are so circular in character as hardly to count as demonstrations.

As I have argued in other contexts, in the Old Testament understanding of history there are three distinct moments or stages characterizing historical passage as Israel experienced that passage. First of all, there was the divine constitution or "creation" of the people and their cultural life. There can be little question that Israel's cultural life had been constituted by Jahweh as probably the paradigmatic act within history of creation: it was God, not they, who established the covenant, who gave the sacred law covering all facets of cultural life, and who even established the political institutions (the judges and later the kings) who governed them. And the main continuing role of Jahweh in relation to this people was the parental one of nurture, fostering, and protection, not so much of individual Hebrews but of the community as a community and the culture as a culture. Israel's culture was, if there ever was one, one explicitly with a "religious substance," one founded directly by God and one preserved and ruled by the divine actions in history. It is appropriate, therefore, to regard as biblical the viewpoint that each creative culture, insofar as it lives on a religious substance, is established in and through the presence of the divine, apprehended or received in different ways than this, as we have seen earlier, but nonetheless grounded there.

The second moment, as we have noted, is the appearance of estrangement or alienation, of the fallen character of even the life of a chosen people. Specifically, this estrangement appears as the betrayal of their covenant, a corruption of the gracious gifts received in and through the creative divine constitution of their communal life. This betrayal and corruption characterized the entire extent of Israel's experienced and recorded life within the covenant, whatever minimal "doctrine" of the fall they might have expressed. As they knew well and repeatedly experienced, the sins of the fathers are visited on their children's children. Thus this alienation was one root, if not *the* root, of the tragic events and ultimately the nemesis that increasingly threatened Israel's existence, as what we call the "prophetic interpretation" of their history makes clear. For she finally came to see this nemesis as God's judgment on her, a judgment so severe and total that it seemed— at least to Isaiah and Ezekiel—to betoken the *un*creation, the unraveling, and the disintegration of the creative culture Jahweh and this people had together raised up. We can hardly say that this experience of the betrayal of *our* creative covenant and this threat of tearing down and even of nemesis are strange to our own experience, either the experience of Western culture generally or that of our own American commonwealth.

The final moment is also prophetic, though it was, so to speak, "signaled" throughout history by Jahweh's frequent and unexpected acts of repentant mercy. This is the promise of a new covenant beyond the destruction of the old, a new creative, redemptive act of Jahweh, the promise of new possibilities in historical life even though the old had now become corrupted, judged, and dismantled. The promise of such a new covenant—of new religious and cultural possibilities—was what provided, in the midst of the experience of social disintegration, hope for the future—though, let us recall, it was rarely welcomed by those currently in power. This theme too finds its echo in our modern experience: confidence in its validity provides the hope so often proclaimed in liberationist movements, and fear of the appearance of the radically new characterizes every "established" or "First World" power, capitalist and socialist alike.

These three moments characteristic of ongoing history as a whole have been drawn from the Hebrew scriptures. They are, as a moment's thought will confirm, expanded, deepened, and refocused around one event or series of events in the New Testament, the life and destiny of Jesus Christ. There divine constitution, divine judgment, and new creative act become incarnation, atonement, and resurrection/*parousia*, aspects of history, to be sure, but not of *ordinary* history. While this deepening and refocusing in the New Testament is central to any Christian interpretation of history, I shall not develop further its implications here. Thus I would like to return to the three moments that delineate a biblical interpretation of the general structure of ongoing history and ask how they illumine for us the contours of our own historical experience. Certainly they are not, as we have seen, totally strange either to ordinary experience of history or even to ordinary views of history. In what, then, does their difference consist? and what does this difference or uniqueness add to our understanding of history and to our *praxis* within it? What we shall find, I think, is that on the one hand each of these three moments—divine constitution, divine judgment, and divine restitution or renewal—appears in its biblical form as apparently increasingly *incredible;* it is a truth about history and ourselves that is steadily more difficult to recognize and, to be honest, which we don't *want* to recognize. Still, on the other hand, we shall see that a closer and more careful look at the real situation shows each to be increasingly validated by that real situation.

Every creative movement or epoch in history believes in divine constitution. It may not put it that way; but intrinsic to any communal myth or vision of history is the deep belief that now at last the essential purpose and goal of history has manifested itself embodied in historical community—needless to say, in our community. It is as if the ultimate grain of history has at last revealed itself; the center and goal toward which events had been moving and the pattern that will set the form of subsequent historical life are now plain and embodied in our communal life. Thus Christian nations and empire interpreted themselves in contrast to their pagan, infidel, or heretical contemporaries. Thus had China and Japan alike understood their role or destiny; and, ironically, despite its deliberate repudiation of the sacred, thus did the Enlightenment and its two children interpret themselves: liberal/democratic culture (this *was* the theory of progress) and now most recently Marxism. What distinguished the biblical (and possibly the Chinese) account from those others is that the divine is not regarded as indissolubly bound to the culture or intrinsic to it, however creative it may have been. Rather, here the divine constitution eventuates in a *covenantal* relationship in which betrayal and even abrogation are possible, and in turn which can result in judgment and ultimate repudiation. In other words, the divine creative act has become characterized by a *moral* relationship in which the issue of the justice of the community is crucial to the relationship of the divine and its constituting power to that community. As a new and unexpected dimension of historical life, the norm of justice has become central to history and with it the conceivability and so the possibility of communal self-criticism at the deepest level appears.

Likewise, every culture has the experience of and belief in estrangement, alienation, and guilt. To all cultures, evil is well-nigh pervasive, human life by and large wrongly lived, immorality generally rife, and whatever good there may be vastly precarious and even endangered. To be sure, they have widely differing interpretations of these aspects of historical life and of what makes up good and evil; and each culture locates good and evil in vastly different places. To most cultures, evil lies in those who are deviant from the community and its ethos; and especially it lies in whatever forces are opposed to the community, in other words, "our enemies." Here among the "bad guys," deliberate wrongs are visible, malice and self-interest obviously rule, and thus the presence of real guilt is undeniable. Modern theory, social scientific or Marxist, tends to dismiss guilt as a false category, itself expressive only of sociological or psychological alienation. On the other hand, modern politics, domestic or international, is as replete with it and with the moral judgments that lie back of it as was that of any epoch.

Again, what is unique about the biblical interpretation of this aspect of history is that the pervasiveness of evil, of moral wrong and thus of guilt, is made universal or all-inclusive. Thus—and here surely is the crucial point—it includes *us* as well as the enemy, the good guys as well as the bad. Clearly a new sort of communal self-understanding that can be self-critical here, and a new sort of transcendence, a self-understanding that can be self-critical and still affirm its own destiny, and a transcendence that yet remains constitutive of the creative value and the potential moral health of the historical community. The biblical interpretation is becoming increasingly strange and incredible to ordinary wisdom, and yet—as we promised—more and more in tune with the actual contours of concrete historical experience.

In a sense too, hope is universal, at least wherever a culture or a community is on the rise, feels itself to be gaining strength, and thus finds itself facing a brightening future. However, despair and hopelessness are in the same sense universal. For the historical forces that impel a movement forward can also—and frequently do—desert it or turn against it; or, as we have noted, it may well bring about its own nemesis. Confidence in liberalism and Marxism alike have waned for our generations. Each in its own way seems to many of it adherents spent as a historical force, its glowing possibilities corrupted into sordid actuality and its theories contradicted by too many historical facts. In such a situation, promise or hope for the future, which is required for creative political action, seems impossible, and as a consequence, forces representing only the past or only sheer power move to the center of the stage. To believe in new possiblities in the midst of an apparently desperate situation, a situation with no possibilities, is therefore almost impossible; existentially, the promise of a new covenant can be quite incredible. Such belief depends not only on a confidence in the sovereign forces of history, but also requires a mode of transcendence in the object of faith of which few visions of history are capable. Such a situation seemed itself incredible short decades ago; but such may well become our situation in the near future.

The uniqueness of biblical hope, however, is not only that it promises new possibilities in even the darkest hours. It is also that what we can genuinely and creatively hope for is not necessarily what we expect or even count on. It is a genuinely new possibility, upsetting and even contradicting what *we* are as well as what our opponents are, against *us* as good Democrats as well as against them as bad Republicans or Communists! Again, transcendence has creatively entered the scene and made all the difference. But because the divine remains constant, it is a new covenant in continuity with the old that we have experienced and loved, and thus a valid object of our hope for the future. The cultural epoch that follows the demise of ours will not follow what either Washington or Moscow or Peking wants; of that we may be certain. And thus is the biblical view seemingly obvious. But because it is the same Lord that rules the future and its possibilities, we may face that promise of the unknown with confidence and hope. And this, I suspect, is at the moment both the most incredible and the most important of all the biblical words of history to us.

2.

Historical Study and the Historical Dimension of Our World

C. T. McIntire

WHAT IS this history we seek to understand? In this age of ongoing historical crisis in our civilization, the question comes to us forcibly in many forms. Can we overcome the legacy of wars, narcissism, poverty, environmental waste, and exploitation? Can we be masters in our own house? Must we contemplate the end of history by nuclear war in our times? Why can we not live merely for the moment? These and similar questions compel us to think about the larger matters of time and human responsibility in the course of history.

For at least 150 years we have been more historically minded than has any previous culture.[1] We have no difficulty regarding everything as change, evolution, process, and flux. Yet in our times we have clung to absolutes—science, material profit, race, nation, class struggle—that rival any other ultimates in history. In academic disciplines like sociology, psychology, economics, and political science, tensions emerge between process and structure, behavior and system, the static and the changing.[2] In popular culture, there are tensions between change and constancy, revolution and absolute values, which unnerve people and escalate into sizable struggles. If we say that everything is historical, do we know what we mean, and can we account for structure and ultimateness?

In the historical profession itself in recent years, historians have greatly expanded their range of subject matter as if to emphasize programmatically the notion that everything is historical. Partly under the pressure of political and social movements and partly just because the matters are there to be studied, the list of types of histories practiced gets longer—women's history, black history, population history, oral history, family history, and much more in addition to the traditional historical subjects.[3] What are we studying when we explore the history of something? Must this proliferation of subject matter and methods inevitably produce fragmentation, or are there common features of what it means to be historical which, if understood, may serve to unify and integrate historical studies?

Historical crisis, historically minded people, historical study. Can we identify what it is about phenomena that allows us to use the one

17

word "historical" in referring to them? Can we understand better what it means to be historical?

I make the following suggestions as a proposal for a way of understanding reality, a way of thinking that we may try out to see whether it illuminates what is historical about reality. I offer my proposal as a sketch rather than an argument. It comes from the vantage point of a historian, but also from someone who, with all other people, shares in and experiences the making of ordinary history. I wish to use certain Christian insights which may orient and direct our reflection on things historical—insights concerning our humanity, our unity as creatures with animals, plants, and physical things, our responsibility and cultural task, the character of time, and the course and meaning of history.

Let me sketch my proposal for understanding history line by line. I shall begin by describing the historical dimension of reality as distinguished from two other dimensions. Then I shall describe in some detail the elements of the historical dimension, noting how they pertain to historical study. Finally, I shall describe how knowing about these dimensions and elements may assist people in the process of historical study.

Three Dimensions of Reality: Historical, Structural, Ultimate

Most broadly cast, my proposal is that reality—our world—exists according to three dimensions, which we may call the historical dimension, the structural (or ontic) dimension, and the ultimate dimension.

We commonly refer to reality as a world of time and space—two dimensions. People who share in one of the world religions—Christians, Jews, Moslems, Hindus, and others— commonly add that ours is a spiritual world, a third dimension. Time, space, and spirit— these are in common parlance the symbols that refer to what I am calling the three dimensions of our world. But these symbols are incomplete. The dimension of the symbol time is also a dimension of things coming into being, of renewal, of development, of decline. Likewise, according to the second dimension, our world is more than merely spatial; it has biotic, psychic, social, political, aesthetic, and other functions as well. Regarding the third dimension, secularly minded people may object to the claim that our world is spiritual in the sense of being related to a transcendent reality. But they will perhaps recognize that our world is a realm of good and evil, and that it refers ultimately to something, even if that reference is to itself or to something within reality, such as the means of production or our humanity or reason.

I wish to catch hold of a fuller understanding of these three dimensions of time, space, and spirit. To do this, I shall use the more comprehensive terms *historical, structural* (ontic), and *ultimate.* The three dimensions are not parts of the world, not levels arranged in a hierarchy, not special features next to other features, and not entities. Rather, they are three total ways in which our world and everything in it exists, the three most comprehensive and three mutually irreducible ways in which the world exists. Anything else we may say about our world may be taken as a subpoint under one of these dimensions. To be complete in our description of the existence of our world, we need to refer to all three dimensions and, moreover, understand each dimension with reference to the other two. I regard these as dimensions of reality that permit us to look at and to know reality in three total ways. Our knowledge of these dimensions we may call our historical knowledge, structural (ontic) knowledge, and ultimate knowledge.

To speak candidly, I should note that secularly minded people who are aware that they see the world differently from those who share in one of the world religions or traditional religions tend to see the world as merely two-dimensional and have difficulty seeing the third dimension. I wish to describe all three dimensions in such a way that even secularly minded people may recognize that what I refer to belongs to their own experience as well.

A set of diagrams may help to indicate the three dimensions of reality in a general way. Let this globe symbolize our world or anything within reality, human or nonhuman, that is identifiable, and let us call it a phenomenon:

Then let us fully embrace the whole phenomenon: first, according to its historical dimension, second, its structural demension, and third, its ultimate dimension:

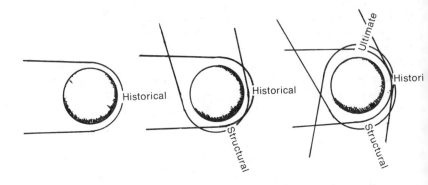

The historical dimension is the phenomenon identifiable as the temporal process of coming into being, carrying on, modifying, perhaps developing, and then passing away. We may describe all phenomena, whether human or nonhuman, as existing in time relationships according to three constitutive processes: first, *becoming*, which involves beginning and integrating; second, *being*, which involves continuing as integral with modifications, including in some cases developing; and third, *ceasing to be*, which involves disintegrating and ending. The phenomenon coheres historically by continuing in existence from moment to moment. What we call the history of something is the actual temporal course of the phenomenon in its becoming, being, and ceasing. The historical dimension thus discloses two elements: 1) time and 2) becoming, being, and ceasing to be. Humans and human products manifest the second element by means of "culture-making"; by this term I refer to human existence as historically creative.

Historical study focuses on phenomena according to their historical dimension. It offers to describe, analyze, and explain in what way and why any particular phenomena or types of phenomena temporally came into being, carried on or are carrying on with modifications, and, if appropriate, have ceased to exist. In historical study we unavoidably assume and deal with the structural and ultimate dimensions, but we do so by means of seeking to understand our subject matter historically. Therefore, historical study is an encompassing enterprise that examines anything in a total way as historical. However, by means of historical study we cannot manage to exhaust what can be studied, and we cannot successfully maintain a claim that what we examine is understandable solely in historical terms, for there are two other dimensions to take into account.

The structural (or ontic) dimension of a phenomenon is the phenomenon identifiable as a structure or system existing with a particular inner constitution or make-up. The structure has parts—like the chemistry and the legs of an insect, or like the legislature and laws of a parliamentary state. By its structure the phenomenon exhibits characteristics such as soft, intelligent, or complex. In its structure it is multifunctional either as a subject or as an object—for example, confessional, political, social, aesthetic, biophysical, and other functions. The phenomenon coheres structurally by keeping its parts, characteristics, and functions in proper relationship and working order.

Various academic disciplines examine primarily the structural dimension of phenomena. Ontology within philosophy is a study of general structures, or of universals;[4] sociology is in part a study of the structure and patterns of behavior of social class and other social relations and activities; economics examines the structure of economic phenomena; and so on. Scholars in such studies cannot avoid dealing with the historical and ultimate dimensions of their subject matter, but they do so as integral to their efforts to focus on understanding general structure, social structures, behavior patterns, and the like.

The ultimate dimension of a phenomenon is the phenomenon identifiable as a manifestation of the meaning of reality and as a disclosure of good and evil, alienation and liberation, sin and salvation. These ultimate matters appear very concretely as the relatively broken or wholesome existence of something, whether human or nonhuman. The ultimate dimension involves disclosing an original as well as final reference by which all else in the universe is understood. The reference may be a transcendent or spiritual one, as it is for Christians to God through Christ, or for Advaita Hindus to Brahman via meditation. The reference may be nontranscendent—to humanity or reason or material growth—as it is for secular-minded humanists, rationalists, or capitalists. In human experience we encounter this ultimate reference in our religions and secular ideologies and in the moral and normative decisions we make and seek to implement in our personal and social existence. According to Christian understanding, reality coheres ultimately as God's creation, maintained by Christ; and Christians are called to work for the coming of the rule of God in the totality of everyday existence.[5]

We emphasize the ultimate dimension of phenomena in religious studies, theology, and ethics, but also in our normative exploration in any field when we ask what is beneficial and valuable for the existence of whatever it is that we may wish to analyze. To do this, we undoubtedly also take the historical and structural dimensions into account.

As this sketch of the three dimensions of our existence indicates, it is true enough to say that everything is historical. When saying that, however, we may add instantly that everything is not merely historical. My proposal entails realizing that the identity of anything is manifest according to all three dimensions, and not by only one or two. For example, historicism tends to make excessive claims for the historical course and process of existence, while secularism tends to deny that anything at all exhibits the third dimension of ultimateness. The study of history depends upon knowledge of the structures and ultimate meanings of the subject matter investigated as we concentrate on analyzing and explaining the historical course and character of our subject.

If we now have in mind the meaning of "historical" in distinction from—but in accordance with—structures and ultimateness, we may turn directly to the historical dimension of existence and describe the two primary elements, namely 1) time and 2) becoming, being, and ceasing, notably as expressed by the creative means of human culture-making. The two elements may not be separated from each other, but we may distinguish them from each other, indicating one and then the other. I shall discuss these elements in relation to historical study.

Time

When I suggest that time is one of two elements of the historical dimension, I should make it clear from the start that I refer to more than the clocks and calendars by which we measure the physical movement of the earth around the sun. I refer, rather, to three features of time that belong to the historical character of our existence. Let me describe the three features, keeping in mind that we concern ourselves with a coherence that may not be broken but that may be approached via one of several avenues. I shall try to include most of the terms people have used to refer to time, and use them myself in describing how they might relate to each other about time.[6] By observing that time is properly included within the focus of historical study, I wish to join historians like Marc Bloch, Eric Hobsbawn, and François Furet, who make time central to their definition of historical study.[7] I hope to benefit from the encouragement Robert Berkhofer gave us to seek to understand why time is so important for historical study.[8]

Perhaps we may gain entrée to an understanding of time if we observe, as the first feature, that time is process. Reality exists as the ongoing, unavoidable, and irreversible course of things. We call to mind the images of movement, stream, path, passage, and line that have recurred in so many of the world's cultures. If we cut short our discussion here, we may be tempted to regard time as mere flux, but there is more to it. Following Judaeo-Christian insight, we may affirm that the ongoing process began with the creation of the cosmos and carries irresistibly onward toward an end, the *eschaton*, which is the consummation of all things and which is already referentially in view. Understood in this way, the process character of time, rather than being mere flux, is one primary way of orienting ourselves to the totality of the cosmos. We live between the beginning and the end, en route toward the *eschaton.*

We may distinguish process from progress: not all process is progress. The term *process* refers to time as ongoing; the term *progress* refers to process that is moving toward a desired goal or in a direction considered good. Processing toward the *eschaton* is progress for the people of God but not progress for those who reject God. Many eighteenth-century Europeans and North Americans believed that history as such was moving irresistibly toward the perfection of humanity; they confused progress with process. Students may make progress in their studies, both in gaining insight and in completing them. Or social revolution in some African country may make progress in lessening social oppression. Whether process becomes progress in the world is relative to whatever goal or direction those in process have before them.

Time as ongoing process is continuous, since the onwardness of things from beginning to end is one unbroken process. We may say that time lasts, that things endure, that the cosmos is one ongoing duration. The temporal continuity of reality from beginning to end is a constituent of the ongoing identity of any thing. Because of time, things hold together for more than a moment.

We experience the ongoing process character of time as occurrences and events. An occurrence is quite literally a coursing of something, something happening temporally. Similarly, an event is literally a forthcoming (from Latin *evenire,* to come out). Occurrence and event are near synonyms deriving from different but related images of time. They are both units of the time-process, demarcated by some beginning and some ending, and possessing inner temporal coherence. A phase, a stage, a period, an age, and an epoch are other such units of time-process.

We can measure time-process by dating with reference to the annual movement of the earth around the sun. Different cultures reckon the start of the dating sequence from different events—the Romans from the founding for Rome, the Jews from the creation of the world, Islam from Mohammed's *Hegira,* Christians from the birth of Christ. Tribal cultures, however, commonly calculate time according to stages or phases of phenomena and events—the daily rhythm of caring for cattle, the seasonal rhythm of planting through to harvest, for example.[9] Whatever the method, such marking of the passing of time-process is essential to the coherence of our historical understanding.

We do not know that time is one ongoing and continuous process from beginning to end by means of empirical observation. The end has not yet come, and we were not present at the beginning. Christians claim to know it by divine revelation mediated by the scriptures of the Old and New Testaments of the Judaeo-Christian traditions. The current physical and biological theories in Western civilization about the origins of the cosmos and life-forms depend on the legacy of biblical revelation that there is an origin at all. The *Puranas,* such as the *Vishnu Purana,* in the Hindu tradition, offer an opposite understanding: that the temporal cosmos has no absolute beginning and no ending either. *Samsara* is an everlasting round of births and deaths of people and worlds.

With the biblical insight, we may believe that anything that occurs in time is unique: it happens only once. Strictly speaking, it does not happen again—that is, all over again. Everything occurs for the first time only. In the Christian view, as expressed by Paul in *Romans,* Christ lived and died only once, and it is unthinkable that he should do it all over again. This was the insight that led Augustine to develop his Christian interpretation of world history.[10] By contrast, Hindus and Buddhists understand time as a process of rebirths, picturing the Atman being born all over again repeatedly in new dwellings until achieving release from the realm of births and deaths.[11] Further, in the Christian view, time-process is not a matter of eternal return outward from a pristine, primordial epoch and back to that epoch again, like tracing a finger completely around the rim of a wheel. In the biblical imagery, we move from Eden as a garden onward to the new earth as a city, the New Jerusalem. The New Jerusalem is not the original Paradise revisited but the perfected fulfillment of the whole intervening course of history.[12]

There is an important qualifier. While it is true that the ongoing character of time means that each occurrence is unique, it does not mean that each is one of a kind. Each event is unique, but it is also similar to others of its kind. Here we speak of events and occurrences as comparable with each other. For example, each sunrise is unique, but each belongs to a set of occurrences known as sunrises; each opening of a parliament is unique, but similar in kind to other such parliamentary events. We also speak of occurrences relating to other occurrences such that they form a sequence of phases that are recognizable as a pattern more than once in history. Each harvest time is the final phase of a series of annual phases beginning with planting time. Shakespeare wrote of "the seven ages of man," and Erik Erikson, in a classic essay, systematized what occurrences are proper to each phase of our personal life history. Others identify stages common to political revolutions or economic development.[13] We frequently speak of liturgical cycles, business cycles, and learning cycles.

We have a habit of regarding the uniqueness and the similarity of kinds of events as opposite. We use geometric images to contrast linear with cyclical views of history, commonly defining Christian views as linear and Hindu views, for example, as cyclical.[14] It would be more accurate, I should think, to say that both Christian and Hindu views account for the uniqueness and similarity of events, but do so in differing ways. For example, Christians understand history, in part, as cycles of distortion and renewal, while Hindus see temporal existence as a linear path of the Atman toward *moksa*. We may understand the uniqueness and similarity of events as two ways of looking at the same thing. All events are at once both unique and similar to others. Indeed, what we call experience when we say we "learn by experience" indicates that, as we encounter new events in the ongoing course of history, we often have a clue about how to handle them because we underwent similar events earlier in the time-process.

A second feature of time is that it is a three-time relationship of past-present-future. The present is the time when phenomena undergo the time-process, or as we say in the case of humans, when we experience existence; the past is the time of going on that has already occurred; while the future is the time of going on still to come. The phenomena go on "now," but no sooner does the going on occur than it passes, and the phenomena continue to go on. We speak of before, now, and after, and earlier, now, and later—the three-fold time-process as demarcated from the perspective of the phenomena in the passage of time. Our languages are constructed around verb tenses, or times, which reflect and account for the character of time as past-present-future: they built the cathedral in the thirteenth century, they build the bank today, they will build the nuclear power plant next decade.

It is important to affirm that time is a relationship of past-present-future, not, for example, something reducible to a succession of points on a graph line in which one point is fully separable from the other points as self-contained. On such a view, the past would be utterly past, the present self-contained, the future utterly future. By contrast, the relationship is a whole in which at no present moment is past entirely past, nor is future merely in the future. The relationship is a dynamic one, in which at any present moment the past is present in the form of the tendencies and the possibilities for what may occur. The relationship shows up in every person and everything at any time in history. I am who I am this present moment partly because of the past course of my life. Unless I die now, who I am now will continue to carry me onward into the future. Moreover, right now I make plans and commitments, have hopes and expectations, enter into undertakings and activities that project my future and influence my present as they help draw me into the future. What I say about myself holds (making the appropriate adjustments) for a scribe in ancient Babylon as well as for an immigrant woman in a garment factory in Toronto today. Further, when people initiate a process such as constructing a building, whether it is a pyramid at Giza or the World Trade Center in New York, the process binds together past-present-future—past preparations, materials, and people, with future projections of what it will take to actually complete the building.

We may say that the present is the referential moment from which we look backward or forward in time. The reference is different for every person in every epoch. My present is not the same as Pope Pius IX's present was in 1860. I look from my present back to his present; his present is part of my past, and my present is part of his future. As a historian, I study him not merely as past; I also study him as present, that is, as I can know him through the now present remains, witnesses, and results of his history. I study his past-present-future: I must understand him as one who inherits the papal temporal power from his past and who determines to protect it and perpetuate it into his future. Moreover, through my study of him, I bring him and his work actively into my present, and I project into my future a knowledge and understanding of his work that may be useful in our ongoing course of time. That pertains to my past-present-future: my past-present-future and his past-present-future are related as parts of one historical process.[15]

We humans have many ways in which we ensure that past is not merely past, and that future is not merely future. We keep our past with us by means of our traditions, customs, habits, memory, and structures. These become means of transmitting past experiences and results into the future. We project our future by means of our plans, visions, goals, hopes, expectations, intentions and desires. These serve to direct us in the ongoing course of time. Our processes themselves are transmissions that carry us onward from the past to the future. A process begun has futurative power until it ends.

There is another sense in which past-present-future are a relationship. Sometimes this is more difficult to see. We may speak of past and future as phases in events or processes that are before and after the phase we now experience or examine. I refer to the similarities among *kinds* of events and processes. In this sense we live in cycles. We may see our possible future simultaneous with our present, or even in our own past. We do this by observing others who are farther along in the phases of a kind of event or process similar to the one we are in. All people in all epochs experience this by being born into a world populated by children and adults who are already in the stages of life we ourselves are likely to go through. A two-year-old girl sees in older girls, young women, and old women stages of life that she may reach in her future. This is another way we learn by experience, namely the experience of others. Such experience enables us, in some cases, to estimate, plan, or predict results—we know how certain processes will operate *if* unimpeded. Unless something is done, we can see the future of the starving people in a village by looking at the funeral of those who have already died because of the famine. Unless we change our ways, we can perhaps see the future of Western civilization in the final years of the ancient Roman Empire.[16]

Understanding time as past-present-future relationship has important consequences for how we study history. It means that, contrary to a longstanding wisdom, historical study is *not* simply about the past but about past-present-future. We need to view the people and things we study not as merely in the past but as undergoing the three-time process. For them, their present is an experience of ongoing occurrence. They at once relate backward and forward: they are structured and conditioned by past occurrences, yet they reach forward into their futures. For them and for us, there is past history, current history, and future history, and we study all three.

Furthermore, if we recognize that history writing or history telling is not merely about the past, but about past-present-future, then we may see that all peoples and cultures possess historical accounts about themselves and their temporal existence in the cosmos. These histories may be oral or written, traditional or critical, about past or contemporary events, mythical or chronological. Whatever the case, they are all about past-present-future and their time in it.[17]

A third feature of time is that time is change. In the ongoing relationship of past-present-future, we experience at every moment the transition between what has occurred and what has not yet occurred. This continual transition constitutes change in the cosmos. We may view change from two directions. From one viewpoint, change is the transformation of the present into the past, the past becoming continually by degrees more remotely past. What occurs changes into the irrevocable conditions for what is yet to occur. Viewed the other way around, change is the future becoming the present. Before anything occurs, it is merely a possibility that may be foreseen or unforeseen. Thus the present is the time of change; it is the moment of the new. It is the time when future possibilities change into actual conditions through the medium of occurrence.

Time as change means discontinuity. The ongoing process of time is continuous, but in the course of time each new moment is different from the previous moment. Each new present is the time when what has occurred gives way to what is occurring. In the present, any existing traditions, structures, ways of life, and behaviors may discontinue, and new ones may occur in their stead. Each new occurrence follows in succession.

Change, therefore, is two-sided: it entails the ending of a previous continuity and the beginning of a new continuity. By marking endings and beginnings, we may identify events, processes, phases, stages, periods, and epochs. In this way we fill out the meaning of our dating systems and further measure the time-process. Historical study depends on the keenness with which we do this.

Understanding time as change and the present as the moment of the new is important in order for us to know that existence is not predetermined. It is easy to exaggerate the futurative power of past events and existing traditions and structures, and to neglect the innovative possibilities of the present. And this is one fallacy of conservatism. Because we study things only after they occur, we can easily interpret their temporal course as inevitable. Viewing them in retrospect, we may see them pressing onward from their beginnings to their endings, and we may thereby fail to view them instead as proceeding continuously through present moments of change when the future was open and undetermined. Because of time as change, moreover, phases and stages of processes must be regarded simply as typical possibilities that actually occur only *if* the processes continue unaltered and to their completion. Prediction, in other words, is always qualified by "if things continue unchanged."

From a Christian point of view, understanding time as change is very important on three accounts. First, all the biblical appeals to us to exercise our responsibility depend on there being, in the very process of things, the opportunity for us to act with an open future before us. Second, Christ's claim that he makes all things new and his call to Christians to become new people who act as agents of renewal depend on the present's being the moment of the new. Not only are we able to bring about new things, but we are held responsible to do so when the old is deformed, repressive, and broken. Third, Christian hope rests on time as change and the present as the moment of the new. In eschatological perspective, as Pannenberg suggests, the future is the coming to us of the new.[18]

These three features of time are manifest by means of the variety of existing phenomena. Time does not exist in itself as an entity, and it is not a part of something or an addition to something, although we can recognize and describe the specific time character of anything. Time, as an essential element of the history of anything, appears mediated via the existence of phenomena in as many different ways as there are kinds of phenomena in reality.[19]

In our civilization, the most popular way we think of time is in terms of clocks and calendars; in history books we most readily meet up with time as dates. Clocks and calendars measure what we might call astronomical time, physical time related to the earth's movement around the sun. This is surely an important and primary mode of time, and it serves as a substratum for all other modes of time. By means of astronomical time we experience day and night, the seasons of the year, annual cycles, and, if we include the moon, monthly phases and cycles. By numerical calculation and physical measurements, we may indeed lay out astronomical time as points on a graph. It would be a mistake, however, to regard time as no more than physical time. We would miss the richness of the manifestations of time in our world.

Let me briefly refer to various modes of time to indicate the diversity of time. Biotic time is related to astronomical time but surpasses it in the time of plant, animal, and human biology. Each plant type and animal type has its own inner time. For instance, in Canada's climate impatiens plants flower soon in their cycle and stay in flower all summer, whereas Iris plants have a much shorter flowering time. Human gestation takes about nine months, whereas cats require considerably less time. Psychic time is the slowness of a boring lecture or the phases of our emotions when we learn of the death of a loved one. Logical time appears in premises, which are logically prior to arguments, and conclusions, which are logically after. Linguistic time is manifest in verb tenses. Economic time is the hourly wage and the phases of a Ford automobile production line, in which interior paint must be applied before exterior paint. Musical time is rhythm and beat.[20]

The diversity of time is crucial for historical study. We are burdened by one-sided divisions of history into years, decades, centuries, and millenia. What may be useful as a rule of thumb for periodizing easily obscures the historical reality that each kind of thing exists according to its own time. The point is illustrated by the old saying that nineteenth-century Europe began in 1789 and ended in 1914. Even to single out the French Revolution as crucial for a new period of European history may prevent us from observing the continuities in peasant life or in the patterns of factory production. It is perhaps one of the failings of serial history, one form of quantification, that it works with equal units on the calendar, usually years. By regarding 1748, 1749, and 1750 as equal units, for example, we may easily miss the fact that the relevant events in economic history may be clustered between August 1748 and February 1749 and not occur further until December 1750.[21]

It helps to be more aware of the inner timings of different kinds of things when we carry on our historical studies. For example, it is important to know that Lord Palmerston and Lord John Russell were old men in the final phase of their lives when they governed England in the early 1860s. Aristocratic government was in a late phase in

England then, while British industrial and financial capitalism was in a middle phase of trade expansion and past the initial stages of invention and capital accumulation. By contrast, in 1860 industrialization in central Italy was a long way from even being able to begin, and the papal government was in a phase of administrative disintegration. A great deal of the understanding we seek through historical study depends on our recognizing that different interacting phenomena are at different moments in their own inner timing.

I have already observed that dating things according to astronomically measured calendars is a valid and necessary exercise. But there is more involved. When we date events 1984 or 1860 or 313 Anno Domini, we orient them according to the Incarnation of Jesus Christ. For Christians, such dating is at the same time both a confession of faith and a temporal measurement. Between the common denominator of the astronomical calendar and the all-embracing salvific advent of Christ, we include all the kinds of time that there are in our world and testify to the recreative dynamic of God's work in the world.

The three features of time that I have identified—as process, as past-present-future, as change—that are phenomenally manifest are crucial for us to understand before we proceed further in our discussion of the historical dimension of our world. From a Christian perspective, we may regard time as good: time belongs to the constitution of the cosmos as God created it. We misunderstand the creation story in Genesis if we look upon time as a bondage and a prison of our souls. When we live in keeping with the times appropriate to each phenomenon, and when we live with time and not against it, we may experience time as the blessing it should be. What understanding of time we take to our historical studies will go a long way in shaping how we treat the temporality of the events and phenomena we investigate.

There are many more things to say about time, of course, but perhaps I have sketched enough to give some picture of time. We can move on to the second element.

Becoming, Being, and Ceasing to Be
via Culture-making

The second element of the historical dimension is the becoming, being, and ceasing to be of phenomena. In distinguishing this element from time, we shift our attention to the way in which phenomena, both human and nonhuman, come into existence, modify, and pass away. Just as all things share in manifesting time, so all things share in undergoing becoming, being, and ceasing. Like time, this element is common to humans, animals, plants, and physical things. However, these different kinds of phenomena come into existence and pass away differently. In this sketch I shall concentrate on the human ways of becoming, being, and ceasing to be.

Human phenomena come into being by culture-making and pass away by what we might call culture-unmaking. Human phenomena do not just come into being; we *bring* them into being by our creative acts. In other words, humans create results: personally and socially we make culture. I want to describe this creative process of culture-making by looking at several matters: first, the processes of becoming, being, and ceasing to be, emphasizing the human processes; second, the creative human acts that make the processes happen; third, the factors that contribute to the processes; and fourth, the results that we call culture.

First, the processes. The following symbol may help us:

The process of becoming is the constitutive way in which a phenomenon comes to be identifiable, manifesting its own integrality and coherence. There are two subprocesses: the beginning of a phenomenon and the integration of the phenomenon. The beginning is the first appearance of features or elements of a phenomenon that permit us to recognize or experience that there is a particular phenomenon in the process of becoming. Very often we are able to recognize the beginning only retrospectively, only after we see or experience that a phenomenon exists. Integration is the process of achieving and the achievement of the inner identity, the integrality, of some phenomenon. It now exists with its own history, structure, and ultimate meaning. It appears that the way in which phenomena begin and integrate varies according to three types: some beginnings and/or integrations are relatively instantaneous; others gradual; and others relatively indefinite, although we can experience or observe that beginning and integration do occur or have occurred.

Let me illustrate some of this variety. The becoming process for a human person, I should think, is the time in the womb between conception and birth as a separate, whole person. The beginning is relatively instantaneous. The integration is gradual over a long period, and its completion is usually relatively instantaneous at birth. The becoming process of a law in a parliamentary state is the time from when somebody or some people first thought of the law to its final passage through parliament. The beginning is usually—but not always—gradual; a number of factors and phenomena come together little by little from disparate directions. Integration is usually achieved gradually as the law goes through the process of passing all the appropriate bodies and authorities. The becoming phase of a spoken word is usually relatively instantaneous: the beginning and the integration occur nearly together. And so on with other phenomena. The history of each phenomenon commences at the beginning of the becoming process.

The being process is the process by which the phenomenon continues as an identifiable, integrated phenomenon until such time as it begins to lose its inner coherence and integrality. I pointedly use the term *being* in a verbal sense to denote continuing presence.[22] For example, throughout eleven hundred years, with many ups and downs, great changes, and what turned out to be only temporary interruptions, papal temporal power endured until 1859–1860 and 1870 as an identifiable ecclesiastical monarchy in the States of the Church. From my birth until this day, through all my changes, I continue as the same identifiable person. As long as the phenomena continue, they have a history.

There are many kinds of modifications that may occur in phenomena during the being process without making the phenomena lose their identity. I shall mention only a few. There are, for example, additions, subtractions, amendments, substitutions, differentiations, revisions, improvements, corrections, renewals, reforms, reformations, healings, deformations, distortions, deteriorations, decay, perversions, hurts, and so on. When one of these modifications occurs, the being process becomes a process of, for example, renewal or amendment. These modifications are part of the history of the phenomena.

One kind of modification—development—deserves special mention because of its prominence in treatments of history in Western civilization. Often history is equated with development.[23] By contrast, I should stress that development is only one type of modification that occurs as part of the being process. When it happens, the being process becomes a process of development. Not all human-made phenomena can develop, and those that can do not always develop in the course of their career. Phenomena that do not develop nonetheless continue to exist; they still have a history. When phenomena develop, they undergo modifications which retain the integrality of the phenomena but which elaborate their features and functions, including an alteration or subdividing of existing ones and the addition of new ones, resulting in new and successive achievements of the reintegration of the phenomena. Either a whole phenomenon may develop, or only one or more of its parts, functions, features, or meanings. It is important to note that there are different kinds of development—economic, psychological, ecclesiastical, organic, and so on. If we treat all development as if it were akin to organic development—the growth of a tree, for example— we miss seeing that economic development proceeds differently from organic growth, and we possibly fool ourselves into adopting a deterministic understanding of development. Let me illustrate what I mean by development. Individual cultural phenomena resulting from our working with physical materials do not develop in their being process. Once a fountain pen or an art work is produced as an identifiable phenomenon, it undergoes many changes and has a continuing history, but it does not develop. However, the design of the pen or the method and line of thought involved in Manet's artistry may develop and be reflected in successively produced fountain pens or paintings. The movement in what we today call the French area from a Frankish tribal kingship, to a feudal kingship, to a dynastic monarchy, to a personal monarchy, to a state monarchy represents profound and interrelated transformations from one phenomenon to another; it does not represent the development of a single identifiable phenomenon. Development is not always healthy: it may be positive or negative, or both. The development of the Mafia's organization, of the state bureaucracy in Prussia, of nuclear weapons, or of a mood of depression are developments we may regard as destructive or oppressive.

The ceasing process begins when the identity, the integrality, of the phenomenon begins to be lost, not to be regained, leading to its termination in the course of history. As in the becoming process, we can distinguish two subprocesses: disintegration and ending. The disintegration of a phenomenon refers to the process of the breaking up of its integrality, to its discontinuation as an identifiable whole. Like development—or modifications generally—disintegration may be positive or negative, or both, depending on the case. Ending refers to the disappearance of the phenomenon as a recognizable thing. Some phenomena disintegrate and cease because their existence becomes so distorted that they can continue no longer. Like the becoming process, disintegration and/or ending may be of three types: relatively instantaneous; gradual; or relatively indefinite, although we can know that the phenomenon exists no longer. The ceasing varies according to the character of the phenomena.

To illustrate, we persons cease our earthly existence by dying. If we are assassinated, as were Thomas à Becket and John F. Kennedy, the disintegration and ending occur relatively instantaneously. Otherwise, we may begin disintegration in a way that is relatively indefinable, and our ending may be gradual; in any case, the final ending is relatively instantaneous. Many mural paintings in Florentine churches, by fading and crumbling, began to lose their integrality relatively indefinably, and they came to their end in much the same way. By contrast, a session of a graduate seminar may break up and end relatively instantaneously or indefinably transmute into a bull session in such a way that we only later recognize that the seminar actually ended sometime earlier. The ancient empire of Rome came to an end not in 476 but relatively indefinably, although we can be sure it came to an end; deciding roughly how and when cannot help but be a matter of debate among historians. The words we use to indicate the disintegration and the ending of different phenomena vary enormously. But when phenomena come to their end, their course of history is over.

In the actual history of most phenomena, these processes occur in succession as phases—for example, the Weimar Republic of Germany went through the process of becoming, then being, and finally ceasing. But in many cases phenomena cease abortively before the becoming process is complete—for example, a proposed Sony product line fails to pass the appropriate tests. When the processes do relate as phases, the edges are often blurry as one thing transmutes into something else. Most important, the processes recur countless times as phases within phases in the actual history of any phenomena, layered upon each other, oscillating in complex ways, succeeding and reversing each other. For example, one addition of a new member to the office staff is in itself a process of becoming and being which, however slightly, transforms previous staff relationships into a process of ceasing. The beginning of one thing may entail the ending of something else, just as it may also ensure the ongoing being of yet another thing.

In the second place, we may look at the creative human acts that make these processes happen. The acts are creative in the mundane sense that they are the means by which humans bring things into existence and modify them. Understood in this way, all humans are creative—and not merely the genius few. Human acts are how we express our humanity. All that differentiates us from nonhumans figures in: spirituality, morality, self-consciousness, historical consciousness, loving, speaking, walking erect on two legs, larger brain size, and much more. The acts vary greatly according to the differences in what we make, who is involved, and the times and circumstances. I can call our attention to this variety by referring to the types and number of verbs we use. In English, with parallels in other languages, we have a primary set of verbs of *making* that explicitly and directly refer to the element of bringing into being. I will mention just some: to construct, to produce, to form, to develop, to fashion, to influence, to institute, to erect, to raise, to establish, to set up, to originate, to fabricate, to manufacture, to issue, to breed, to shape, to mold, to give rise to, to restore, to rehabilitate, to leaven, to effect, to pass (a law), and so on. Surrounding these primary terms of *making* there is a wide range of transitive verbs that transmit an action by an agent to the object and imply making. Let me illustrate: to sail the boat is to make the boat move; to write the book to to bring the text of a book into existence. If we broaden our horizon to include intransitive verbs, we find that making is missing as a primary or even a connoted meaning of such words. To show result, we must add a phrase: the woman persisted, and the man finally gave in; our spirits drooped, so we decided to quit; the prices rose—and hurt the people on welfare.

In a Christian perspective, we may understand our creative acts of culture-making as the human means whereby we respond out of our created humanity to the will of God the Creator. In relation to the nonhuman creatures, we humans become creators under God, mediators by whom God continues his work of creation. We humans are made so that we may respond to God according to and in fulfillment of his cultural mandate as disclosed by the creation story in Genesis. Part of our calling is the responsibility to care for the whole cosmos, for ourselves, and for all the other creatures. Our responsibility is to enable the other creatures of God—the rocks, the plants, and the animals—to fulfill their calling in being what God made them to be, to ensure the healthy interrelation of all God's creatures, and to engage in the ongoing process of creativity by bringing things into being, modifying them, and bringing them appropriately to an end. Insofar as we fail in our responsibility, we bring much havoc, evil, oppression, and brokenness into being. Instead of acts that care for ourselves, others, and all creatures, we destroy, exploit, and deform what God made to be good. Acts of culture-making, thus, are deeply spiritual acts in which we are responsible to choose for what is good and to create culture that is a blessing and not a curse.[24]

Third, there are the factors involved in making the processes happen. I use the word "factor" in its radical sense of "maker": that which makes, helps make, participates in making results (Latin *facere*: to do, make). Factors are what go into making results, making things occur in the existence of any phenomenon. Any persons—and any human and nonhuman phenomena—or any of their parts, features, functions, and meanings, are factors when by their interrelating with other phenomena they contribute to making results.

The culture-making process is highly complex and multifactored, even for the most apparently simple things. At every present moment, a high number of factors conjoin to form a configuration of factors by which we humans together tend to bring the phenomena into existence, or to continue and modify them, or to discontinue them. We may distinguish two angles of approach, both of which lead us to discover a multiplicity of factors in action. First, as I have already noted, all phenomena are multifunctional, meaning that while a particular function may define and center a phenomena, other functions cohere in its structure as well. For example, an academic seminar may be a human association characterized by its academic function, but it exercises many other functions as well—social, economic, psychic, confessional, spatial, numerical, and so on. Second, the environment of any phenomena includes a manifold range of other phenomena that interact with the ones we make the subjects of our study. Thus, a graduate seminar at the University of Pennsylvania is the academic center of an ongoing and changing configuration of factors, including the personalities of the seminar members and their life histories, the history department, the university, and the academic world, but also the people of the neighborhood, the economy at large, the various state and federal government departments, the current artistic, musical, symbolic worlds, the military situation, the climate and geography, and so on. The active combination of the multifunctional make-up of any phenomena with the many diverse environmental phenomena means that many different kinds of factors, as well as many particular factors, are at work in the making of anything. The way in which the many factors interact varies according to the case. No one factor or kind of factors is always the most crucial—not the economic, nor the psychological, nor the intellectual-confessional, nor the social, for example. In each case we must find out what factors are most crucial and how they are configured. For example, we may understand the building of a medieval church as a multifactored process of culture-making in which theological and ecclesiastical factors normally centered and provided definition to the process, and in which a vast array of other factors conjoined in the human acts of bringing the particular church into being as well as modifying it over many generations—the materials, the skills and personalities of the laborers, the patrons and patronage, the townspeople, the harvests, the population size, the symbols, and so on. If in the case of a certain church the theological and churchly factors did not serve to center the process, the result achieved, instead of being a church fully suitable for worship and ecclesiastical acts, may be predominantly an artistic monument or a grand memorial to a wealthy family. In such cases we may observe that the artistic or sociopolitical factors have prevailed to the detriment of churchly life. We can analyze the making of any phenomena in analogous ways.

Fourth, we may describe what it is that comes into being, modifies, and passes away—that is, the results of the culture-making process. Our creative acts, in conjunction with many factors, bring into being and sustain results. We may call these results culture. As with the word *time*, current usage of the term *culture* tends to be restricted to what we may regard as only two or three of its forms. In cultural anthropology, the term usually refers to ideation, that is, to the symbols, rules, myths, norms, ideas, and signs that permit us to discern the meaning of human behavior or of human-made objects.[25] The concept is sometimes expanded to include the behavior and the things whose meanings are disclosed by ideation. In everyday language we retain a narrow meaning of culture as having to do with the fine arts and letters, or more narrowly still, with the sophisticated manners of social elites. In these various usages we place the term next to others as if culture were only one aspect of our life, such as in the triad of culture, society, and personality. These usages are further contrasted with the term *nature* as referring chiefly either to the biophysical substratum of humans ("our animal nature") or to the world unspoiled by humans out there in the wild.

The meaning I understand by the term *culture* is more comprehensive than these current usages. I associate the term with literally everything brought into existence by humans, the whole way of life of a people and all its ingredients—not just our indicators of meaning, our arts, or our manners—and with all aspects of our humanity, not just our suprabiophysical characteristics. Culture is the outcome of the creative process as well as the condition of the ongoing process of human creativity. We might say that culture represents the ongoing results of our creative acts. It is important to remember that these results exist in varying degrees of wholesomeness and brokenness, peace and violence, joy and sorrow, good and evil—all due to our relatively healthy or unhealthy acts of culture-making.

The types of cultural phenomena are several. First, we must list ourselves, human beings, as persons. Lest we forget, we are born as a result of fully human acts of procreation, every aspect of which—biochemical, psychosexual, social, ethical, confessional—is a fully human matter. Second, we may list human functions and acts that express our humanity yet result from learning, such as praying, loving, socializing, painting, thinking, speaking, cooking, farming, and so on. Third, there are the societal results, the institutions, associations, and relationships, and their features, like churches, families and friendships, governments, states and city-states, factories and markets, feudal relationships, patron-artist relationships, social classes, tribes, communes, cities, and farms. Fourth, there are the results of our working with animals, plants, and physical things, like domesticated cattle and hybrid roses, meat for eating and wood for building houses, and machines, glass, and art works. Fifth, there are the intangibles, the emotional, mental, and symbolic results, like moods, fears, and joys, ideas, meditations, and beliefs, norms and rules, words, names, signs, and manners, creeds and laws. Sixth, there are the totality results, like societies, peoples, humanity, cultures, and civilizations.

These results of culture-making all have several things in common: they come into being by personal and corporate human acts; they manifest their identity according to the three dimensions of history, structure, and ultimateness; they are comparable to others of their kind and different from those of different kinds; they are variable according to different times and cultures.

It is important to affirm that these cultural phenomena really exist—and that they exist in varying shades of health and unhealth. They are not merely names that we historians and others create; they are not reducible to mere processes; and they are not illusions (*maya*). It is a Christian belief that we are responsible as persons and as communities for what we do and for the results of our acts. I take it to be part of the meaning of this divine call to responsibility that the results of our creative acts really exist and that they can help or harm others.

As with time, Christians may regard becoming, being, and ceasing which proceeds by means of human culture-making as good. We need not believe that the process is meaningless—or a terror. Instead, we may understand it as one by which we carry out our mandate to respond to God through creativity that is healthy and not oppressive. The reality that all phenomena in the cosmos are not in themselves eternal, but come into being, exist in their variable course, and finally cease to exist may be understood as a revelation that all phenomena in God's creation have their appropriate limits of time and being. So long as our acts and their results are healthy, and not harmful, we may gladly understand our responses—along with those of all people in all ages as well as those of the nonhuman creatures of God—as participating in and contributing to the total history of the world from the origins to the *eschaton*. As with time, the understanding of becoming, being, and ceasing that we take to our historical study can deeply affect our treatment of the existence of what we examine.

Perhaps I have said enough to indicate what I mean by becoming, being, and ceasing, especially as it is a result of human culture-making. We have before us now both elements of the historical dimension of our world.

Proceeding with Historical Study

My proposal has sketched in two parts an understanding of historical existence, first as a dimension of our world along with the structural and ultimate dimensions, and second as a dimension composed of two elements: 1) time and 2) becoming, being, and ceasing. Earlier, toward the end of my description of the three dimensions, I noted that we may observe that everything is historical but not merely historical. Now I may add that everything is historical by existing as a temporal process of becoming, being, and ceasing to be.

It is possible to apply this sketch directly to the study of history. To do this, I shall translate what I have described into a sequence of five kinds of questions: the first concerns our choice of subject matter, and the others involve discerning four classes of relationships among the enormous number of details of our subject matter as we proceed in our historical analysis.[26] These relationships correspond to the dimensions and elements I have described.

First are the questions of subject matter summarized by our asking, What shall we study? This requires us to select from out of countless phenomena in the universe some phenomena to the exclusion of others. Once selected, the phenomena themselves directly set requirements and hold out possibilities for what we do. We need different concepts, methods, and sources to appropriate different kinds of phenomena. The variety of types of historical study—for example, women's history, population history—originates in the first instance from differences in subject matter. Once having begun our study, if we shift our attention, however slightly, we actually focus on different subject matter, and we submit ourselves to different requirements, create different concepts and methods, and use different sources. For example, if our subject is Edouard Manet's life, we investigate what is pertinent to a person's history, and we formulate appropriate concepts and methods and seek suitable sources. But if we change our minds and decide to concentrate instead on his impressionist paintings, our requirements change.

The second set of questions are questions of structure. We ask, Who and what parts, functions, and characteristics properly belong together in the structure of our chosen phenomena? Answering these questions leads us to discover many kinds of things, such as: How many of Manet's paintings may be regarded as impressionist? What were the ages, occupations, church affiliations, incomes, places of origin, and destinations of the Dutch immigrants to Canada in the 1950s? How did papal administration work in relation to trade tariffs and merchant activity in the Papal States of the 1860s?

Third are questions of ultimateness. We want to know: What ultimate meanings and orientations did the participants understand and their actions and results disclose? What did they regard as good and evil in the events? What norms did their affirmations, protests, conflicts, and products reveal? In response, we learn things such as: whether the *Bhagavad Gita* speaks of physical or spiritual warfare; whether the framers of the American Constitution aimed to preserve liberty or merely to protect private property; whether the messages conveyed by television advertising reveal the ideology of capitalism.

Fourth, there are questions of time. We ask: When did people and things exist and events occur, and in what time relations and phases?

We learn things such as: whether all the pharaohs of Old Kingdom Egypt continued to build pyramids; what the time sequence of industrial inventions was in eighteenth-century England; how the phases of the capitalist transformation of the Mawri productive system were related to the actual chronology of events.

The fifth group of questions, with reference to human becoming, being, and ceasing, are questions of culture-making. We wish to discover: By what processes did our subject matter come into existence, modify, and, if relevant, cease to be? Who and what were the factors? With such questions we learn: what led Manet to adopt impressionist principles and later to abandon them; what the relative influence was of the cabinet, the queen, the prime minister, and the foreign minister on the making of Tory foreign policy; whether the Lutheran Reformation depended on bourgeois urbanization.

These questions provide a fivefold way of indicating what is historically significant to include in our study. The questions of the selection of subject matter are the most crucial. Once we have made our decision, the historical significance of anything for our study depends thereafter on whether it pertains to our chosen phenomena. The other four sets of questions provide four groups of criteria for further assessing historical significance. Anything is significant if it is especially indicative of the ultimate meaning, the structure, the time, and the factors and processes involved in the coming into being, modifying, and passing away of our chosen phenomena.

These five kinds of questions have a cumulative and transformative impact on our historical study. We need to ask all five questions and learn to ask them creatively and not woodenly. It is good to have them in mind as we pursue our examination. Indeed, it is plausible to think that all five kinds of questions enter into our analysis whether we consciously ask them or not. I would venture the observation that all forms of historical study consciously ask the first, the second, and fourth questions—those concerned with the time and structure of their subject matter. Others add question three. To achieve a fully historical study, however, we need to consciously include question five, the most difficult but properly the destination of our historical analysis. We must at least learn time relationships in the existence or our subject matter in order for us to engage minimally in historical study. But we need to go on as best we can to see our chosen phenomena in the process of coming into being, being, and ceasing to be for our work to be fully historical study.

Having described all this, I am now ready to return to the question that opened this essay: what is this history we seek to understand? Holding our sketch before us, perhaps we may gain a clearer understanding of the way in which our world is historical. Our task remains to use our understanding as, under God, we make our common history from the origins to the *eschaton*.

3. The Difference in Being a Christian and the Difference it Makes—for History

By Martin E. Marty

SOME YEARS ago philosopher Mortimer Adler wrote a book entitled *The Difference of a Man and the Difference It Makes* (Holt, Rinehart and Winston, 1967). His device—"Turing's game" it was called—was to posit a human being behind one curtain and a human-like robot behind another. The robot was computerized to perform humanoid rational functions. One could pose any sort of question to it—and get answers that seemed equivalent to those a human being would return from behind the other curtain. Despite the rough rational equivalency between the two behind-the-curtain entities, Adler found ways to define and affirm the importance of being human through intricacies of argument that have nothing to do with the case before us. His only appearance on the present scene is to provide a device that leads into a question of some importance for Christians who are historians or historians who are Christian, or people who read or listen to them.

What difference does "being a Christian" make, and then, what difference does "being a Christian" make—for history, for the writing of and reflection on historical work? Suppose one were to set up two Adlerian-style curtains and place behind them not an historian and a robot but an historian who is confessingly Christian and one who is professedly not. Assure them both of sufficient sabbatical funds, have lunches brought in to them, and grant them back-door egress so no one in front of the curtain could ever see the two, read their labels, see who wore a cross, or use any other means to learn how the two are identified.

To continue the experiment, assign each the same topic in Christian history. For example, get them a grant to write on the Synod of Quiercy of 849. (Picture the good old days when the Canada Council or the National Endowment for the Humanities was willing to fund humanistic ventures that were not immediately "relevant.") Let both historians pursue the sources wherever they might lead, bring in all the historical methods and insights one learns in the academy, engage in the hermeneutics of suspicion, and then craft a narrative about how under Hincmar of Reims the Synod condemned Gottschalk of the too-rigorous Augustinians, banishing him to the dungeons of Hautvillers.

Some day, these being well-chosen and productive historians of the sort that endorsers recommend to councils and endowments, each issues forth an elegant historical monograph. Could one by reading it see any difference "being a Christian" would make? If so, how? If not, why would "being a Christian" ever make any difference to the historian? Is the Augustinian theme too irrelevant? Should the scholars have been given a more delicate subject? What about two historians who deal with biblical materials, who are assigned the story of the burning bush, the revelation on Sinai, or the resurrection of Jesus. Hypothesize, at least, that the Christian, like many other scholarly Christians, has a firm faith in the God of the Christian faith and a firm grasp of historical methods. She or he couples these with an internalization of the reality—as she or he sees it—that the documents telling these stories have their own human historical dimension and can be subjected to critical analysis. Would their stories necessarily differ? Might they? Are there not many Christians who can live with more-or-less naturalistic explanations of ancient events recorded in Scripture? Do not many non-Christians have such empathy for the biblical world view that they can write effectively and with authenticity, "from within," as it were, "the inner history" of events that other nonbelieving historians may treat "from without," as "external history"? If so, is "the difference" between the two a matter of the *Verständnis* and *Vernunft,* the comprehension and discernment that psychologically astute historians seek on any subject?

Finally a paragraph must arrive in which one stops enjoying the luxury of piling on questions—but the pile-up of such questions has served a purpose. Very seldom do members of the craft reflect on the difference their faith or nonfaith makes in the production and understanding of historical work as *historians* measure it. This is at first glance rather strange. One has little difficulty spotting a Marxian interpretation of history, whether it shows up in grand-scale philosophy of history and deals with the future, with outcomes, or only in workaday-world narratives. It would be hard to miss the Marxian assumptions of an E. P. Thompson in his work *The Making of the English Working Class.* Where Marx fails Thompson, Freud helps him out both in the *Vorverständnis,* the "pre-understanding" he brings to evangelical and Methodist piety, and the "post-understanding," or conclusions he draws from his subjects' actions.[1] What hermeneuticians call "the agent's description"[2] is wholly absent from Thompson's treatment of the hymns they sang. What to them was a word of piety and truth in a hymn that begins, "O precious side-hole's cavity, I want to spend my life in thee . . ." is to Thompson a Freudian womb allusion couched in a Marxian dulling of revolutionary fury and a distracting with the opiate of religion.

Similarly, it is difficult to disguise—and one is even forbidden to explain away—the difference being a woman makes in writing "women's history" or the difference being a black makes in writing "black history." When one announces his or her assumptions as a "psychohistorian," there is a license to "see" in events what may otherwise miss the eye. Thus Erikson, in the best-known case, does not need to take Martin Luther's theological ideas as seriously as he takes his bowels and bathroom habits.[3] Similarly, idealist assumptions show up in the exposition of history by idealists: they look for something different, cherish something different, and expound something different than do those historians who ignore or oppose their philosophical outlook. Why, it may be asked, should all these be privileged in the academy, and why should Christianity alone be an embarrassment, a hard-to-isolate dimension, a voided mark of distinction?

The Difference in Being a Christian

It would be foolish to try to define what being a Christian is in all its scope. Even the most rudimentary definition gives away whole schemes of background commitments concerning the nature of being a Christian. Thus, to say that it means to be grasped by "the new being in Christ" is to state the reality as it has been transmitted (and traduced, some would say) by Platonists, idealists, Schellingites, and Tillichians on Christian soil. To have one's restless heart quieted by having found its rest in the God of Christian faith adds a psychological and Augustinian dimension at once, neither of which will be fully acceptable elsewhere. To the Christian moralist in the tradition of the canonical Epistle of James, the difference in being a Christian has to show up sooner or later, preferably sooner, in conduct, in ethical patterning and behavior.

For our present purposes, these extensions and elaborations can be bracketed. When the issue of studying and writing history is concerned, one can evade and postpone such issues and concentrate on the central theme in interpretation. To be a Chrisitan in this context is to construe reality in a particular set of ways through the prism provided by witness to the activity of God, especially as seen in Jesus Christ. However one elaborates that vision, evading the interpretation or construction of reality that coheres around Jesus Christ would keep one outside the Christian orbit. One is free to tamper, of course, but this produces conceptual impropriety and linguistic nonsense on a scale that Lewis Carroll's characters alone could love. G. K. Chesterton—probably, at least, it was he—is said to have said that one may draw a long-legged, long-necked yellow mammal with brown spots and under the picture write "alligator." But this is likely to cause confusion to those who have learned to connect the word "giraffe" with such a visual image. So to evade the construing of reality through the figure, event, memory-impression, or image of Jesus Christ would be some sort of mislabeling, however clever its sleight of hand may be. Some minimal truth in packaging has to be present if people are to communicate responsibly.

This extremely broad definition of the difference being a Christian makes in the world of interpretation may be relatively noncontroversial. The difficulties come in when one examines "the particular set of ways" one construes reality. Having pointed, then, to the difference in general such a commitment makes for any believer, we have the project that is more difficult to focus still ahead: what difference does this difference make for *history*?

The Difference for a Substantive Philosopher of History

The most simple case for any sort of distance relates to being an historian who is a substantive philosopher of history. To many working historians that is a contradiction in terms, and one can almost hear over his shoulder the scolding of the giant Jacob Burckhardt: "Above all, we have nothing to do with the philosophy of history. The philosophy of history is a centaur, a contradiction in terms, for history coordinates, and hence is unphilosophical, while philosophy subordinates, and hence is unhistorical."[4] So it may be, but the fact remains that many historians engage in substantive philosophy of history and their work is reviewed in journals of history or taught in classes on history, in the Christian sphere as well as elsewhere.

The best clue to the substantive case is in titles of books. One begins to sense and smell its presence whenever a book includes the word "meaning" in the title. Such books flood to mind at once: Nicholas Berdyaev, *The Meaning of History;* Martin D'Arcy, S.J., *The Meaning and Matter of History: A Christian View;* Karl Löwith, *Meaning in History;* Henri-Irèneé Marrou, *The Meaning of History* are samples from an ample trove.[5] To them one can add many titles that do not claim to expound the meaning of history but do so, among them H. Christopher Dawson's *The Dynamics of World History.*[6] On a different scale is Arnold Toynbee's *A Study of History,*[7] which purports to be historical and certainly pays attention to mountains of historical detail but which "knows" something of where civilization(s) and history are going. And in a different genre, if one can picture paleontology and its projections through evolutionary time-scales as history—which in some senses it is—Pierre Teilhard de Chardin was a substantive philosopher of history dealing with an "Omega Point" in Christ, an event that had not yet occurred but had a bearing on the construing of all events that led up to it.[8]

Arthur J. Danto has provided a convenient approach to distinguishing substantive philosophy of history from its analytic counterpart, or from the writing of "ordinary" history. "Substantive philosophers of history, like historians, are concerned to give accounts of what happened in the past," writes Danto, "though they are concerned to do something more than just that." He continues: "The difference . . . between history and a philosophy of history cannot be that the latter gives, as the former does not, accounts based on detailed factual findings. For such accounts are given by history and philosophy of history alike." Instead, as Karl Löwith has written, substantive philosophy of history is "a systematic interpretation of universal history in accordance with a principle by which historical events and successions are unified and directed towards an ultimate meaning." The trigger word here again is "meaning," a word that alerts us to something special going on. Danto agrees that it signals something "essentially theological," or at least that it has "structural features in common with theological readings of history," which is something that even Marx and Engels the atheists saw, for they read history through "essentially theological spectacles" even though they did not find a divine play or divine being.

Substantive philosophy of history "is a certain *kind* of statement about the future . . . an *historical* statement about the future." Thus it is connected indeed with ordinary history. Historians and philosophers of history alike ponder the significance of events, but "philosophers of history seek for the significance of events before the later events, in connection with which the former *acquires* significance, have happened." There is, adds Danto, "no context wider than the whole of history in which the whole of history can be located." Danto thinks that substantive philosophy of history is a mistake, a misconception about the logic of tenses; but this is a point that need not concern us when we are not talking about the logic of tenses. It is important here simply to note the presence of a significant enterprise and industry, from Augustine to the already mentioned moderns who deal with the past as part of the whole. That whole implies some sort of previsioning of a future, an outcome, a final vantage from which one appraises events in the past and the present that would otherwise be unintelligible or that would, in any case, lack "meaning."[9]

Substantive philosophers of history may raise problems for analytic philosophers like Danto or for ordinary working historians who concern themselves little, if at all, with the philosophical issues. But they exist, are productive, have followings, and impart sorts of meaning.

They often belong in at least the margins of the historical fraternities and sororities and attend their scholarly gatherings. Many a conventional historian can go through decades of a career disguising her or his sense of meanings and then, when elected to the presidency of an association or invited to moonlight with published memoirs, suddenly spills out a cosmic backdrop to the empirical and mundane work that had preceded. They at least merit discussion in the not always polite company of ordinary historians.

In the conspectus of the question concerning the difference that being a Christian makes, it is obvious that here Christian faith and outlook make enormous differences in the work of such historians, if it is granted that they dare also be called historians. The tests are not foolproof. Mortimer Adler did not have to cope with the issue of hypocritical robots or inauthentic humans behind the curtain; but someone who wishes to be both neat and rigorous about our test must do so. It is possible for someone called Christian, who construes the whole of history "in Christ"—as Christians for all their modesty about knowledge and the future must—to be acting in bad faith, either as a phony or as someone who has not taken issues seriously enough to explore his or her attachment to their possible truth claims or falsifiability. Similarly, it is possible that a nonbeliever, an outsider, may by extraordinary ambition and scholarly sympathy for the subject matter move beyond a psychological identification with his or her characters or themes to the point that he or she may dedicate a career to a Christian substantive philosophy of history. Ordinarily, however, such a person tends to make clear a sense of limits: this kind of thinker makes no higher claim than to give a fair and honest reading of how other people who believed the Christian story conceived the future. Most vocational substantive philosophers of history are motivated to make impassioned claims for the truth of that meaning as they see it, however modest they may be about the visibility of that meaning or the potential agreement over it in the larger community of believers.

Analytical Philosophy of History
and Ordinary History

One would be ill-advised to hang out a shingle as a lifelong worker in the "meaning" field without having deep commitment to that meaning. But the motivation for other ways of looking at the past need ask for no such commitment at all in order to promote staying power. When I was a graduate student, a friend was working on "the self-diffusion of liquid sodium." Another scientist happened by his laboratory one day as we were visiting and, having heard what material my friend was working with, blurted out, "That's a damn interesting substance!" If that can be said of liquid sodium, it can be billboarded and megaphoned with respect to people who take the shoes off their feet on holy ground, claim to have greeted someone risen from the dead, engaged in jihad or crusade or inquisition, or handled snakes without being bitten. The substance of their history is damn interesting, perhaps more interesting than railroad history or labor history or the story of roofing technology in Virginia's past. So the writing of ordinary religious history attracts the talent of many who stand outside the claims of faith, and these may often have more durability and finesse than do many insiders. It is no secret, for instance, that William McLoughlin, by most critics' consent the foremost if not also the most controversial historian of revivalism in the United States today, both stands outside the circle of those who claim the truth of being "born again" and writes circles around most of those inside that orbit.[10] There are no creedal tests in the history departments where the vast majority of religious historians are trained, and while childhood religious exposure may often go into the package of predispositions and motivations, there is no reason to believe that historians of religiousness and religious phenomena score significantly higher than do other academics in church attendance, private prayer, or other affective dimensions of religiosity.

Place the non-Christian and Christian behind two screens and have each pursue that Synod of Quiercy or the Presbyterian Schism of 1837: will one necessarily be able to see the Christian commitment emerge in the second case? *No.* That one word takes suspense out of the rest of this essay, but it does not close the window to issues of interest. The working historian or "analytic philosopher of history" may and, in my reading of things, necessarily must come with many preconceptions and commitments, many of them religious or quasi-religious, creedal or semiconfessional. Even the most positivist historians can be exposed by clever sniffers for metaphysics, exposed as being burdened or informed by metaphysical outlooks. But they may make systematic efforts to carry as light a burden as possible, to be as chaste about metaphysical informing as they can be.

In Danto's terms, with Burckhardt, the analytical philosopher of history only "co-ordinates" events that are "temporally distant from one another, . . . respectively past and future to each other, though both past to the historian." The analytical historian and the ordinary working historian may find meanings in their stories in the light of some projection of a future, but it may belong to their self-understanding to bracket or purge these as consistently as possible, especially when these are called to their attention. This may be deucedly difficult to do, and to the rigorous seekerout of metaphysical codes and signals it may be finally impossible. But in this as in other professions, the professors must at least be given the chance to act on a certain logic of conviction and a would-be consistency of practice. "Historians, *as* historians," writes Danto, "are not concerned with events in *their* future, or at least not concerned with them in the way in which they are concerned with events in their past. . . ." Thucydides is considered the father of scientific history because he was chaste about the logic of tenses and the limits of meaning by someone who as a writer interrupts the stream of events somewhere between past and present. So long as one does so, it is difficult to tell from the story itself what investment the historian has in the meaning of history, meaning the *whole* of history, including the future—which, for Marxist and Christian alike, belongs to the story.[11]

Analytical Philosophy, Ordinary History, and Verification

To be as pointed as possible about "the difference," let me argue here that the ordinary working historian or analytical philosopher of history, by the canons of the profession—if we want to label giraffes giraffes and alligators alligators—has no tool for breaking what I call "the confining circle of immanence" on historical grounds at all. He or she may faithfully chronicle the experience of people who claim to have recognized the invasion of the transcendent into the sphere of the immanent, the infinite into the orb of the finite, the divine inside the human world. But ordinary historians are always called up by the ethics of their profession and the watchful scrutiny of their colleagues to produce documentation of the way they deal with the "traces" left by events in the past. Further than these traces their researches cannot carry them.[12]

Here one may keep the argument chopped clear by saying that the ordinary historian, subject to the canons of what historians mean by history, is required to perform something analogous to what the language philosopher calls "empirical verifiation." When one cannot do this, his or her work will be categorized in a different way: it may be apologetics or proclamation of a kerygma; it may be prophecy or poetry or philosophy of history. On these terms, the meaning and truth of theological discourse "from within," as it were, is eliminated and scorned. Such a would-be historian steps beyond saying "this or that set of people witnessed to the existence of God acting in their history." If the claim goes further, it falls to any number of empirical choppings, like that of A. J. Ayer, whose approach is usually billed as "classic":

> If the sentence "God exists" entails no more than that certain types of phenomena occur in certain sequences, then to assert the existence of a god will be simply equivalent to asserting that there

is the requisite regularity in nature; and no religious man would admit that this was all he intended to assert in asserting the existence of a god.[13]

As with existence, so with event—with happening. To say "God acted in history in the call of Israel in exodus or the endurance of exile" is to make a sentence that cannot be verified logically or following the meaning of tenses. First of all, the event is simply lost. The historian was not there. Had he been there, how would one verify that the voice that was heard, the pillar that was seen, the pull that was felt was God's and not a trick? In the Christian scheme, whatever the object may be that one wheels out on stage for ordinary empirical verification of the sort that impresses historians cannot, in the very nature of the case, be the God who is God beyond the gods. We have only reached the first stage of questioning that critical history must do: what was the event? Already the difficulty is insuperable *if* one's goal is to "prove" or "verify" the existence and intervention of God in history, something the Christian "believes" occurred.

The second stage is not insuperable, but it is full of problems, as anyone who has followed two hundred years of critical historical analysis will know. That is, how reliable is the trace? The traces we have are the existence of a people who felt called or, in the Christian case, who claimed the experience of the Resurrection. We know about this through the continuity of a story-telling community, and we find a regulation or assurance of some "sameness" in the telling through a canonical Sripture. This may be seen as a "revelation" of God, but to make that claim again throws one into the whole set of issues that empirical verification establishes for and around historical inquiry. This is not to say that "truth" is dependent on the temporally approved and passing paradigms of an academic profession, but only that we have to find a different name for the profession that claims to prove the truth of the revelation and, behind the documents that preserve it, the verifiable reality of a hidden God made unambiguously manifest in this or that happening. On those terms only, that is, if a Christian historian could have the means of "pulling rank" and effectively demonstrating the truth of this happening as revealed in these traces, would being a Christian help—so long as this "historical" game is the only one that is played. As with ordinary history, so with analytical philosophy of history: the game seems to be over, with little potential for the historian or history.

Bonus Differences that Being a Christian Makes

From here on, one is involved with a retrieval. Having argued that "being a Christian" can make an important difference of a qualitative character in contention for a substantive philosophy of history, one notes that such a qualitative difference is not demonstrably present in the case of analytic philosophy or critical history, where different standards of verification are more rigorously applied. It is shaky to make a rationale for the Christian as historian from a retreat position arguing that the Christian at least brings quantitative superiority. And it is similarly shaky to argue, in parallel fashion, that a choir of Catholic converts or born-again Baptists may or will, because of their commitment, do a better job of singing a Bach oratorio that is somehow premised on faith or directed to supporting the faith community as well as entertaining a hall of concertgoers. The Sunday painter who "believes in Jesus" is not necessarily or even likely able to match the assertive and aesthetic power of an impassioned nonbeliever who brings painterly skills. Abbé Paul Couturier did the French Catholic community a favor in announcing that he trusted genius more than faith when he called upon architects and artists to give powerful expression to the languages and images of the community in a new day.

So critics would regard as pious prattle or foolish pride whatever would lead Christian historians to claim that, despite their limits as historical detectives or prose stylists, their writings are better than those of people who stand outside the circle of faith but who have great gifts and arts of empathy for those within it. The "difference in being a Christian" has more to do with the *vocation* of an historian than with the production of a particular monograph or even *oeuvre*. The collectivity of people inside the churches who worry about the topics of the past, who confront the church with the value of the story and the academy with the value of the church's story, acquires a value in a world where "everybody's job is nobody's job." They of all people have the burden of keeping the language of Athens and Jerusalem before each other. Through refinement of their vocation—in part by their bringing together of the concerns of substantive and analytic philosophies of history, critical faith and critical history—they can bring gifts that are recognizable in a church that often does not heed those gifts, or in an academy that may ignore both certain topics and certain nuances. Such a claim would be as uninteresting to the Mortimer Adler standing before the two shrouding curtains as it would be to the A. J. Ayer standing before two sets of propositions for verification or to the Arthur J. Danto examining two understandings of historical traces in the light of the logic of tenses. It represents quite a retreat from either the qualitative or quantitative claims.

Fortunately, life is not lived within only Adlerian, Ayerian, or Arthurian Dantoesque "rules of the game" or verificative tests. In philosophy, any number of Christian theologians have pointed to "the manifold logic of theism," for example by employing functional instead of verificational analysis. They ask what language is out to perform in its communal context. As Frederick Ferré has argued and reminded, a different model for language usage now comes into play: *"Language . . . is a complex social product with many legitimate uses."* So "the task of functional analysis is both to elucidate the meaning of language by revealing its use or uses in context and to uncover linguistic misuses when they occur." He develops topics that are not of moment to this point, since his concern is with the community of philosophical language, not historical analysis. Alongside "the logic of verificational analysis," he shows the functions of the "logic of analogy," the "logic of obedience," the "logic of encounter." In no case does Ferré disguise the sense of loss felt when chasteners of linguistic logic in propositions found it impossible to engage in verificational analysis. But on the table there left bare he has brought other modest gifts.[14]

This historians can also do by concentrating on Christian themes imposed on them by their faith commitments in their "Athenian," not their "Jerusalemic," communities of discourse.

One instance of the gift the believing historian brings to the Athenian or academic circle is his or her motivation—and, one hopes, talent—at "smoking out" the presuppositions others bring. In the language of thieves and thievery, "It takes one to know one." Someone who comes with a Christian "philosophy of history" appears first as an embarrassment, then as an outrage, and finally as a creative diagnostician if he or she is capable of eliciting from others a concern about the commitments they bring to any historical work that many of them would previously have described as "merely empirical." These philosophies, these visions of "meaning in history" or "the meaning of history," may, for example, be Marxist, progressive, or nihilist. In each case the Christian can ask, "How do you know the meaning? How do you know to make the judgment? How do you assess value *as historian* without having a hold on the whole of history, the only vantage possible, and to have that without knowing something of events in the future, the certainly impossible vantage for analytical or critical historians?

Christian historians, more positively, have worked for centuries with some vision or other of Providence as the guiding hand, only to see it replaced by Progress, and finally by the chaos of modern pluralism. In the midst of the symbolic confusion that results when no two symbol systems seem to intersect and when mere solipsism threatens, Christians can at the very least point to the God-shaped blank on the void or desert of human history and indicate the processes by which people, through language appropriate in the light of "functional analysis," saw purpose and meaning. This language may have been emotive or performative or whatever; the point is, it functioned to give life and purpose to specific communities. Where one cannot have progress one can at least have process. Where a whole society cannot agree on the outlines of history—as, putatively, ancient Israel or medieval Catholic Europe did—they can at least move from confusion to disagreement and on occasion to some measures of minimal consensus, thanks to the pressing and urging of Christians. They at least know what common faith means in the life of a people.[15] They have no monopoly on this pressing and pressuring, but they have the longest set of reasons in the Western world to speak of canons and confessions, consensus and common faith.

Third, a difference that being a Christian means for being an historian shows up in the creative juxtaposition in life for one who claims "God exists" and yet that "God is hidden." (Let us not get lost for now in the meanings of "God exists" and its cognates; let's be content simply to say that at least the Christian sentences and stories— in the world of giraffe-giraffes and not alligator-giraffes—does not regularly permit "non-God" in the center of its experiences and propositions.) In the modern world, life at this juncture is more painful than ever before; but Augustine earlier worried about it, as did Job long before. Martin Luther in the Heidelberg Disputation warred against "contemplative" theology, the "theology of glory," where speculators claimed to peer into the divine majesty. He called instead for a contentment with the theology of the cross, an historical understanding, which seeks whatever meanings are accessible not by staring at God head-on but by being content with the *posteriora dei*, the "hind parts of God," God's always hidden, partly mysterious, and necessarily ambiguous traces in human history.[16]

Fourth, the Christian in the historical community is committed, whether or not he or she lives up to that commitment, to be a discerner of the first lineaments of "the new creation" inside the old. This does not mean that Christian historians can deal with texts from the past and find that the new always wins out. There is no disguising the death of innocents, the victimization of the more faithful people, the demise through death and suffering of those who had no special burden of guilt but on whom towers of Siloam fall. Yet the Christian reads and must read these texts as potential disclosures of many modes of being, and is motivated to keep seeking discernments of the new creation. This approach gives, or should give, tremendous staying power to the Christian as historian. It should liberate him or her to take care for the mundane. On this point, Martin Luther can serve as a witness, for a second time not because he would have ever satisfied anyone abiding by the canons of critical history—which was not then yet invented. Instead, his was a critical theology that witnessed to the traces of God but saw them as *larvae Dei*, masks open to many interpretations. Yet

Luther spelled out a reason for critical attentiveness in mundane history:

> For because histories describe nothing other than God's work—
> that is grace and wrath—which one must so worthily believe as if
> they stood in the Bible, they should certainly be written with the
> greatest diligence, faithfulness, and truth.[17]

The Difference in the Christian Community

The working historian or the analytical philosopher of history may feel as ignored and irrelevant to the Christian company as Dylan Thomas's poet is to lovers lying abed not needing or knowing his poetry. Yet in an interactive Christian community, the historian has his or her own modest gifts to bear, if there can be a hearing and this hearing is met with some eloquence. One need only mention here some of the gifts the historian by vocation can bring.

Historians point to the validity of the earthly enterprise. Even Augustine in *Civitas Dei*, while pointing to the ephemerality and corruption of the earthly city, had to tell its story and honor it with loving attention to detail. Most Christian historians in Augustine's wake have been less nervous about wallowing in the particulars of mundane life, and thus they serve as balances or as checks against those who would denigrate or dissolve history through radical eschatologisms, docetism, angelism, or anything else that counters the biblical texts calling for an endowment of the temporal venture with meaning.

The historian in the Christian community can, in the terms of the Adolf Harnacks and Ernst Troeltsches, help the community "overcome history with history." Critical history can be used to demystify the spell of tradition where that is burdensome and can liberate people from time-bound forms that acquire their power by looking eternal. Exposing false decretals and pointing to the accidental and contingent character of events that the community too readily sacralizes and idolizes are part of the historians' vocation.

They can, further, serve the believing community—and often, by indirection, the surrounding culture—by offering it models. Historians' work that may be intrinsically valuable becomes extrinsically relevant when society, which has no memory, "stops to think."[18] By keeping the records fresh and ample, the historians can enlarge the repository of options for people in traditions gone stale. Thus, in the Second Vatican Council, when it was clear that triumphalist and fortress models were no longer appropriate or effective, the historians (who were often biblical scholars) came forth with models of the "servant church," the "pilgrim church" or, especially, not the hierarchical mystical body but "the people of God."

Even the utopian has no models to draw upon but those made intelligible by their partial and preliminary existence in other conjunctions in the past. At the same time, those who present models for the future can also be creative dispellers of Utopia. When the Christian community unwittingly adopts a metaphysic of Progress, the historian can point to failed Utopias of the past and can at least raise abrasive questions about too ready acceptance of new panaceas for all of history.

One could extend such a list indefinitely, but its purpose is to be suggestive, not exhaustive in the catalogue sense. It is to indicate that while Christians cannot meet the ordinary canons of critical or analytical history when they make claims for verification of a transcendent intrusion in the human past, they have many other gifts to offer. If they retain a sense of Christian vocation, they should themselves never run out of an agenda or grow bored, even as they should not give their fellow believers premature or superficial peace.

4. Common Sense and the Spiritual Vision of History

GEORGE MARSDEN

In early 1966, shortly after I finished graduate school, I visited two graduate school friends of mine who had landed attractive positions at California Institute of Technology in Pasadena. Their history department, they said, had spent the entire fall discussing the question of what their purpose was in teaching history at a technical school in southern California. None of the traditional ideals seemed to fit what they were actually doing. Finally they came to a formula they could agree on: the purpose was to teach the students to vote Democratic.

Perhaps it is clear enough that the ultimate goals of Christians teaching history differ substantially from those so perceptively summarized by my friends—perhaps for some it is not so clear. In any case, I think that we all have at times been faced with the more general issue that such discussions raise. How much does our academic work really have in common with that of our non-Christian colleagues? This is a persistent question for twentieth-century Christian academics. Each of us has been trained in a non-Christian graduate school and licensed with a Ph.D. to practice his or her specialized art or science. The profession has its own rules and standards for technical proficiency. When we actually do history (as distinguished from using it to carry out some hidden agenda like getting people to vote Democratic or to become missionaries), does our Christianity really make a substantial difference? Should my Christian profession substantially set off what I do in my classrooms or my scholarly publications from what my non-Christian colleagues do? The answer to this question bears not only on the profession of history but on other academic disciplines as well.

In viewing the relationships between Christian and non-Christian history, we can discern two contrasting experiences that seem common. On the one hand, it seems to many of us that in principle a Christian perspective on history should make a vast difference. Much has been said on the subject, and if one surveys the bibliographies on Christian views of history, one begins to get a sense of the staggering volume of recent literature.[1] If history is understood through the lens of Scripture, it seems to take on completely new dimensions affecting everything from the question of what the facts are to grand schemes about historical significance.

Yet, another phenomenon seems equally common. Much of the

history that we do turns out to be not much different from what is done
by our secular colleagues. In fact, with a few exceptions, there seems to
be an inverse relationship between how Christian a bit of history is
and how good it is as history. If Christian motives are obtrusive, or if a
hidden Christian agenda is uncovered, Christian and non-Christian
historians alike usually will agree that—again, with a few exceptions—
it is bad history. Such observations have led many Christian historians
to argue that the best way to be a Christian historian is simply to be a
good historian, though occasionally adding some essays specifically for
Christian audiences. In any case, the discipline of history has a basic
set of rules on which Christian perspectives should not intrude.

In this paper I want to try to cast some light on these well-worn
issues by looking at them as questions in epistemology—as questions
in how we know and think about things generally. Although this is a
philosophical issue, I am convinced that no theory of history is worth
much if it is not an outgrowth of principles we are familiar with in our
everyday experience. History is, after all, an extension into the past of
our attempts to make sense out of our everyday experience. So while
this approach is philosophical, I trust it will not be especially abstruse.

In twentieth-century thought there are some powerful strains that
suggest that perspective, and hence Christian perspective, should make
an immense difference. Probably in no field have these strains been
felt more strongly than in history. Already in the first half of the century,
the brilliant Carl Becker articulated the critical importance of this point
of view. Becker started with everyday experience but interpreted it in
the light of philosophical pragmatism. For all practical purposes, said
Becker, the past exists only as our ideas of it; otherwise it is gone
forever. Accordingly, the facts of the past do not speak for themselves;
but we understand them only in the interpretive framework of the ideas
we already hold. So, differing world views, differing interpretive models,
differing purposes for thinking about the past make even "the facts"
appear differently for differing groups of people.[2]

Such ideas, long familiar among historians, have recently been
popularized in other discipines, especially with the vogue of Thomas
Kuhn, who applied them to the seemingly strongest bailiwick of objectivity, the natural sciences. In Kuhn's view, what is science for one
group may seem nonsense to another; what are crucial data to some
scientists look irrelevant to others. Fundamentally differing paradigms
separate competing groups of theorists from each other, and communication across these paradigms is often virtually impossible. They
operate with differing languages—with differing conceptualizations
and meanings they give to the "data."[3]

Christian theoreticians may readily adapt aspects of these views in
order to claim that Christian perspectives should make a vast difference.

I, at least, have argued this way. Based on a synthesis of ideas from Becker and Cornelius Van Til, I have argued that the very facts of history differ for the Christian and the non-Christian historian. There is, in this sense, nothing like objective history. Even when we see things like trees, we see not simply natural objects but creations of God— expressions of his creative wisdom. More importantly for historical work, we see humans not simply as natural objects but as creations of God in his own image.[4]

I still think that this view is correct; but I think there is also something misleading about it. It seems not to account very well for a large part of our experience—and a large part of our experience as historians. In fact, Christians and non-Christians see the same thing when they see a tree or another person. In fact, in doing history, Christians and non-Christians often find large areas of commonality in their understanding of the past. So I want to look also at the other side, the side that accounts for the experiences and understanding that we have in common with our non-Christian colleagues.

Here again, I want to start with everyday experience, but this time with what I find to be the very helpful suggestions of the eighteenth-century philosopher Thomas Reid, founder of the Common Sense school of thought. (Reid, it is worth mentioning, held many views that Becker, in *The Heavenly City of the Eighteenth-Century Philosophers,* claimed were no longer viable.) Reid was concerned to answer the skepticism of his countryman David Hume. Human knowledge, Reid argued, actually stands on a firm foundation: the common sense of mankind. Virtually all normal adults find that they are endowed with certain intellectual mechanisms that force them to hold certain beliefs. For instance, virtually everyone is forced to believe in the existence of the external world, in the continuity of one's self from one day to the next, in the connection between past and present, in the existence of other persons, in the connections between causes and effects, and (given the right conditions) in the reliability of their senses and of their reasoning. None of these basic beliefs is based on reasoning itself, Reid said. We simply find ourselves with belief-producing mechanisms that induce us to hold them. Attempts at demonstrations of such beliefs are superfluous, since we have nothing more sure than these mechanisms themselves as our access to the truth.[5] In practice, normal humans simply find it almost impossible not to rely on these basic means of gaining access to knowledge. Only philosophers and crackpots, Reid was fond of saying, would seriously argue against the reliability of these first principles. And even skeptical philosophers duck when they go through low doorways. So do Hindu mystics.

Two such truth-conducive mechanisms in particular are as essential to history as they are to everyday life. Our dispositions (under certain conditions) to believe our memories and (under certain conditions) to believe the testimony of others often lead us reliably toward the truth.[6] Everyone knows, of course, that neither of these belief-producing mechanisms is wholly reliable. Just as surely, however, no normal adult can cease entirely to rely on these mechanisms as means to get access to the real world. Often we are justifiably sure of things that are matters of recent memory; the same applies to some knowledge gained exclusively by reliance on testimony. In all cultures throughout history, courts of law have relied on such evidence, even in matters of life and death. Almost all our knowledge of the past before our own lifetime relies on testimony. Yet we may be almost as certain as the fact that we are sitting here that Cleopatra existed, even though we have little reason for this belief other than the evidence of testimony.

Reid's conception of our knowledge of the past differs markedly from that of many twentieth-century views. Becker, for instance, insisted that when we know the past we know an *idea* about the past; the past as such is gone forever. What we are left with is history or *ideas* of the past, and these ideas, of course, exist in the present. So we lack access to the events that underlie the records we have of them.[7] Kuhn develops a more thoroughgoing skepticism as to our ability to know about things themselves, apart from our theories about them. "There is," he says, ". . . no theory-independent way to reconstruct phrases like 'really there': the notion of a match between the ontology of a theory and its 'real' counterpart in nature now seems to me illusive in principle."[8]

Twentieth-century thought is riddled with such assertions about our inability to get at reality except in the form of our ideas or theories about it. Nowhere has this view been more pervasive than in modern biblical studies, especially outside evangelicalism. Probably the strongest theme in such scholarship has been that we do not have access to the biblical events themselves but only to the apostolic or prophetic kerygma or faith concerning those events.[9] In mundane history also there are tendencies, by those preoccupied with historiography, for instance, to treat history as simply interpretation. In such views the past becomes a sort of Rorschach test in which we read projections of our immediate interests.

Such views, as plausible as they are, ultimately end us up in a morass of subjectivism. Thomas Reid, impelled by David Hume to anticipate these issues, observed that only theory is on the side of the subjectivistic and skeptical conclusions. In practice, no one can really believe that he can not know something of reality itself, and no one can live as though he believed that. The problems, said Reid, arise from the theory of ideas, popularized by John Locke. Locke suggested that ideas of the external world are imprinted on our minds through our senses. Our knowledge of the external world is thus mediated by these ideas, which are the direct or immediate objects of our thought. Hume pointed out the problem—still with us—that we have no way to tell that our ideas correspond to reality. Reid answered simply that if we discard the philosophical concept of "ideas" and start with common sense, the problems are resolved. Common sense tells us that we can know directly something of reality itself. Our direct knowledge is not confined just to our ideas, which are in our minds, but involves what is really "out there."

Reid's views, it seems to me, help clear up some troublesome questions concerning historical knowledge. Just as in everyday life common sense leads us to believe that we know something of the real world "out there," so it tells us also that we have some direct access to the past and not just to our present ideas about it. Moreover, we are virtually forced to believe, and to act on the belief, that other people have similar knowledge. Although philosophical speculations might suggest the contrary, we do in fact have some theory-independent access to events in the past. Some such knowledge cuts across all theories and paradigms, and it provides all people of good sense a solid reality basis for testing some aspects of theories. So in practice there is a common ground of historical inquiry. When we look at the past, if we do it right, what we find will in large measure correspond to what other historians find.

From a Christian perspective, we may explain this phenomenon simply by observing that God in his grace seems to have created human minds with some abilities to experience and know something of the real world, including the past. Furthermore, these structures are substantially common to all normal people so that, despite the notorious theoretical problems of subjectivism and point of view, we can in fact communicate remarkably well and be assured that we are talking about the same things. It may be difficult to explain, except as a matter of faith, what basis we have for reliance on these common abilities; but the fact remains that only philosophers and crackpots can long deny that often they are reliable.

When Carl Becker and his twentieth-century colleagues rejected such eighteenth-century formulations, they were reacting to a combination of two emphases that happened to be inextricably intertwined. Especially in American thought, common-sense philosophy was thoroughly wedded to "Baconian" confidence in the scientific method. Many nineteenth-century thinkers, as well as many early twentieth-century scientists and social scientists, vastly overestimated the possibilities for obtaining objective results by following correct scientific procedures. Twentieth-century thinkers such as Becker and Kuhn, who have rejected such illusions, have in the process written off the common-sense foundations of human thought and communication as well.

Clearly, however, common sense and "Baconian" objectivism need not stand or fall together. One can, for instance, maintain that we share with the race common sense abilities to know something truly of the real world "out there." Nonetheless, we might always be perceiving it dimly and with some distortions of cultural and personal bias.

I find this relationship clarified by a metaphor: I picture our access to reality as limited by a series of lenses much like the multiple-lens glasses that eye doctors test us with. Each person wears a different series of lenses of biases and prejudices. Nonetheless, all normal people still read many of the same letters on the chart.

But what then of our radical Christian perspective of which we talk so much? Is this just rhetoric that amounts to little more than wearing rose-colored lenses when we do what everyone else does? Or perhaps in effect we believe that our Christian glasses add a new area to our vision. We see not only the letters that everyone else sees but some others, spiritual ones, as well. These extra areas, however, do not much affect our vision of everyday experience, except perhaps occasionally to create a halo effect. Or perhaps, more strongly, these extra beliefs operate as a "control" on our everyday common-sense beliefs, so that no common-sense belief that we have may contradict one of these extraspiritual beliefs.[10]

These images, although helpful, do not seem strong enough to me. Their weakness, I think, is that they seem to presuppose models for our intellectual activities that are too exclusively mechanical. We add one set of beliefs to another, and the one set colors, shades, or limits the beliefs we hold in the other set. Perhaps even occasionally a belief in one area provides some input for beliefs in other areas. The relationships, however, are conceived as essentially mechanical ones resulting from additions or beliefs.

I think we can cast some more light on these relationships if we consider a slightly different model of how the mind operates. Here again, I begin with some suggestions from Thomas Reid. Reid pointed out that our basic beliefs are not based on arguments. We do not believe in things like the existence of the external world or other minds on the basis of calculations of the evidences or inferences from arguments. Rather, the human mind as it matures develops natural abilities simply to read "natural signs" or "natural language."[11] Some of these abilities to "read" the signs of the external world are learned—for example, we learn to associate a certain smell with roses. Yet even in such cases, the intuitive sensibilities of the mind to make sense out of our experience often go beyond what can be accounted for by the mechanics of logical calculation. The clearest example, I think, is the marvelous ability of three-year-olds to learn the most complex lan-

guages. Somehow they have an intuitive grasp of complicated relationships that go far beyond their logical abilities to make inferences.

Such intuitive organizing abilities, I think, are the chief qualities
that distinguish human thought from computer intelligence. Computers, for instance, despite their immense logical powers, find it impossible to translate languages well. Much of what we understand about
reality is not reducible to a set of rules.

The human mind, then, seems to be endowed with remarkable
potential to intuitively organize its experience—to see patterns in it.
Some of this pattern-seeing we hold in common with all normal people.
We all perceive trees and ducks and other physical objects in certain
shapes familiar to the whole race. In more complex aspects of experience, however, this immediate pattern-seeing may vary substantially
across cultures or professions. Some premodern peoples might not
have been able to perceive that the dots on a television screen represent real peole. Or a space technician may be able to perceive an event
from a glance at a board that looks to the rest of us as just a set of dials
and guages. Related phenomena are illustrated by the famous Gestalt
examples of the double picture, where one or the other or both of two
objects may be seen.[12]

In such cases it becomes clear that we do not see the patterns by
calculating logically or mechanically from the evidence. Rather, our
seeing of it is triggered by a few clues. Some people may be unable to
perceive one of the pictures, but if a few clues are pointed out—the

chin is the nose—they will suddenly see the whole picture. Similar cases abound in our experience. Bach or Mozart may be playing, but many people may perceive no harmony in them. Yet if someone were to point out to them the proper things to listen for, or perhaps if they were put in the company of those who appreciated such music and so listened to it with new ears, they might intuitively come to sense the beauty. In a sense, such appreciation is learned; yet clearly the intuitions for seeing the beauty that is there go beyond anything that we are taught or that we learn simply through conditioning or in computer-like or mechanical fashion.

The central point of this essay is that the epistemological implications of the Christian's knowledge of God are clarified if we consider them as analogous to these everyday experiences. In the light of this analogy, some of the paradoxes associated with a Christian perspective—as in one sense seeing everything differently than does the non-Christian, yet both of us seeing many of the identical things that are "really there"—are not unique or as problematical as they might at first seem. Rather, they are much like similar—and readily understandable—phenomena of our everyday experience.

Consider first the analogies between such everyday experiences and our experience of knowing God. The world is filled with the language of God, with the signs of God that the heavens declare, much as a room might be filled with the music of Bach or Mozart. Many people, however, may fail to sense the harmonies and the beauties of these expressions of God's love. If they come to appreciate such harmonies, it likely will not be because they have heard airtight arguments demonstrating their existence. Little of what we know is arrived at by such argumentation. Rather, they begin to read properly the signs and clues of God's presence. The arguments may help, just as a course in music appreciation may help one appreciate Bach. But other ways of coming to see the signs may be more decisive. We may be in the company of believers who lead us to look more carefully. We may hear a sermon. Or we may just look at the starry heavens above and the moral law within, and all of a sudden see that what the Bible says is true. It comes to us as an earth-shattering insight, not as the result of a calculation. We now perceive quite clearly a pattern in reality that we had not seen before.

Historians should have little difficulty appreciating this account of learning to know God, since it is analogous to our experiences of gaining historical insights—save for the earth-shattering quality. Historical breakthroughs are made not by simply assembling the evidence and making inferences from it, but (since the evidence itself is often overwhelming, amorphous, or seemingly contradictory) by insight that sees some pattern in it. Of course, it is essential to discover the fact and to get them straight; but anyone who has read a lot of Ph.D. dissertations knows well what history is like without insight. With the insight, all sorts of things suddenly fall into place. The Jacksonians' backward-looking Jeffersonian-agrarian rhetoric masked forward-looking capitalistic aspirations. Americans' tolerance of slavery reflected "the dynamic of unopposed capitalism." The American colonies were becoming more Anglicized as the Revolution approached.

The discovery of the new pattern, of course, does not change the facts; rather, it forces us to see the known facts in a new light. The facts may appear in some new relationships to each other, and some facts that were previously considered unimportant and overlooked now assume new roles and new prominence. Moreover, more than one pattern of insight may account well for the phenomena in question. Arthur Schlesinger, Jr. saw the New Deal in essential continuity with the great tradition of American reform; Richard Hofstadter saw it as a pragmatic "new departure"; radical historians of the sixties saw it simply as an effort to preserve capitalism at the expense of neglect of oppressed classes. Each group, however, when they did their work responsibly, cast light on what is perceptibly the same corpus of facts.

So it is with distinctly Christian views of history. When we add the Christian lens (the lens of Scripture and spiritual insight) to the other lenses through which we view reality, several things happen. Not only does the new lens color what else we see and add new areas of beliefs that act as controls on our other beliefs; it also provides clues that allow us to see new patterns of relationships among our beliefs. As in the Gestalt shift between seeing the two pictures, biblical and spiritual insights allow us to reorganize our intuitive grasp of the patterns in our experience. As in the case of the Gestalt shift, however, there is a sense in which we continue to see precisely the same "facts" as the person who views them in the alternative pattern. Each of us sees the same black lines with white spaces of a certain size between them. Common sense survives as a basis for understanding and communication, despite our differences in overall perception. To be sure, the perceptions of the different patterns may make an immense difference: what one person calls a nose the other person insists is a chin. Nonetheless, common sense plus a little effort in sympathetic understanding can assure us that in an important sense we are talking about exactly the same thing.

If we apply such models to explaining relationships between Christian and non-Christian scholarship, we find that a number of seemingly perplexing relationships appear not much different than phenomena common in our everyday experience. Accordingly, we can distinguish at least four different ways of relating the two kinds of scholarship that nonetheless are no less compatible with each other than are similar varieties within our aspects of our knowing.

1) First, we should expect that in many of the details of our scholarship, when we are working on technical aspects of a problem or discipline, what we will do will be virtually identical to what non-Christian scholars might do. In the Gestalt double-picture analogy, we might agree thoroughly on technical questions such as the distances between one black spot and the others. Or we might run a quantitative study on a section of the picture to determine the ratio of black to white. In such technical work we should expect no difference between Christian and non-Christian work. In some academic disciplines, such as physics, most of our work may involve such technical questions. In history these are less pervasive, but they still form a large part of the academic enterprise.

2) Another way that this model helps account for substantial commonality is that it suggests that even when one *is able* to see strikingly new patterns of relationships, one does not always *have* to see the patterns in the new way. Our powers of sympathetic understanding aid us in being able to view the same data in more than one pattern of relationships; we can shift from one pattern to another. So for certain academic purposes—for example, presenting to the *American Historical Review* our account of the relationships of church and state in Fascist Italy—we might adopt a stance and language in many respects similar to that of our professional colleagues. Again, our common professional and technical interests in getting the story straight may for the moment outweigh our concern to specify how the events fit in the larger patterns of God's relationship to the world. In this regard, it should be noted that while Christians possess the abilities to see the larger patterns of relationships through biblical and spiritual lenses, sometimes they simply fail to do so, even when they should. With apologies to the perfectionists among us, our noetic sanctification is no more complete or consistent than is the rest of our sanctification. Hence we can account for some of the commonality simply as the result of our spiritual sloth. Other commonality, as I have emphasized, is quite legitimately due to our limiting ourselves, for technical or professional purposes, to discussing only certain patterns.

3) Sometimes, however, our biblical and spiritual lenses should change our views of our technical work. As we have already noted, Christian beliefs should provide a control on our beliefs arrived at through other sources. So if our technical work has led us to conclude that human history has no meaning, direction, or purpose, we ought to re-examine the assumptions out of which such conclusions grew. Furthermore, if we are seeing the overall picture in a reorganized pattern, that will change the way we value certain details of the pattern. This

will particularly change some of the questions we ask about the data. If we perceive that the supposed chin is really a nose, we will ask different questions about it; we will view as important some details of the picture that others overlooked as simply incidental. So if we view the Catholic Church in Italy as not only a powerful political force but also as an agency sometimes used by God for great good, or at other times used by people for great ill, we will sometimes ask different questions about it and thus doubtless notice some things that our non-Christian colleagues overlook. Such differing insights may make substantial differences in the interpretative directions our technical historical study takes. For instance, we Christians see human beings as responsible agents, but not in sovereign control of their own destinies. We see deep defects in human nature and judge it by standards of morality that may differ from non-Christian views. Human freedom, so highly valued of late, is not ultimate; it is destructive unless combined with a sense of dependence. We see through the common human illusion that people control their destiny by wealth, power, or cultural achievement. Their very accomplishments in such areas may become their vices, especially if severed from the spiritual sense of dependence. Accordingly, we do not accept the view of humanity common among many social and behavioral scientists—that with proper adjustment most of our social-cultural problems can be resolved. The perceptions of such patterns in reality can or should reshape much of our historical inquiry.

4) Finally, there are aspects of seeing through biblical and spiritual lenses the overall patterns that are extremely valuable and radical simply in themselves but that do not carry very directly into much of our professional academic work. Often the broadest insights are both the most important and the least practical academically. Again I think of the case of physics. It is most important for the Christian physicist to recognize that the entire physical world is an expression of the creative power of God. Yet this all-important insight that changes everything one sees might change little in the physicist's career of technical investigation. Similarly, in the case of the Gestalt pictures, the most important thing about the Gestalt shift is that in a sense the relationship of *everything* changes. Lines that once were seen as representing an old lady now represent a young one. But this most important insight may be most important just because it is an overall insight, not because it translates into something that changes our views in smaller perspectives. Of course, as emphasized in point 3, in some areas the overall shift does make very practical differences.

In conclusion, recognizing these varieties in the ways the shift may relate to our academic work, let us look more specifically at the overall new pattern of a biblical and spiritual view of history. If we view history—or reality generally—through the lenses of Scripture and spiritual insight, we will see in reality clues to its spiritual patterns and dimensions. These clues are the language of God: the presence in creation of all sorts of signs of his creative activity; the presence in history of his redemptive work; and the sense in our hearts of our own inadequacy and sinfulness and need to trust in God. Such clues awaken in us a new intuitive perception—or at least the ability to perceive—of a new order in reality.

As far as history is concerned, this new perception should awaken in us a sense that the real dynamics in history are spiritual. History is not just the story of the human will, though undeniably that is what we study primarily. Yet this human story takes place in a larger context— in the context of a larger struggle among real spiritual forces and personalities. For Christians themselves, such sensitivities may be of practical importance, as I think Richard Lovelace has shown well in his *Dynamics of Spiritual Life*.[13] On the other hand, they may translate into professional historical work only in some indirect, though perhaps important, ways.

My own understanding of this dimension has been helped a great deal by thinking of our situation as analogous to that of the characters in the sagas of Tolkien. Great spiritual forces play awesome roles in history. We can only dimly perceive and fathom the dimensions of these forces. Yet we do have some guides. We do not know the outcome of any particular battle with the forces of evil; yet we have assurance (though it sometimes dims) that in the end good will triumph. Our role is nonetheless crucial. Somebody must carry out the missions that bring history to its appointed place. If we do not, someone else will be raised up who will. So, frail as we are and weak before these gigantic forces, we must nonetheless do our best. Ultimately, we know that our doing is not a matter simply of our efforts but of some higher grace. Nonetheless, we humans *do* play important roles as responsible agents. In one sense the course of history rests in our hands, even though in another sense we know that it is controlled by higher spiritual powers.

In order fully to appreciate the force of this overview, we have to go beyond the model for human understanding that I have been presenting. The spiritual view that I have been sketching as most important in reorganizing our experiences is essentially in the tradition of Augustine, Jonathan Edwards, and Abraham Kuyper. I have been trying to relate this view, however, to more technical, practical, everyday, and common-sense aspects of understanding that influence our academic work. In the Anglo-American traditions, at least, this latter outlook has been associated with the Baconian, inductive, empirical, and Common Sense traditions. These two types of traditions, I think, can be put together more easily if one is willing to recognize the phenomena of Gestalt-type shifts in our understanding, so that often we shift from seeing things in one framework to seeing them in a quite different one. So contradictions between the two views may be only apparent.

The two traditions, however, differ substantially in their conceptions of knowledge, and ultimately we must be clear on which is more important. In the Augustinian tradition, knowledge has been characteristically related to one's affections—to one's loves. Love of God then conditions one's knowledge of God's creation. In the other tradition, more characteristic of the modern scientific outlook, knowlege typically has been viewed in more abstract terms. We know propositions that are conceived abstractly as true or false statements.

In much of American academia in the past one hundred years, this latter ideal for truth and knowledge has triumphed. The triumph is, I think, part of the general advance of technological ideals in our civilization—part of the triumph of "how" over "why." In academia the triumph was marked by the development of the Ph.D. dissertation as the license for entry into the discipline. The ideal is that of becoming an expert—of knowing about something that no one else knows about—and of applying scientific methods to this knowing. Even in history, where positive science is severely limited, this ideal has had a major impact. Our knowing, if not simply of true and false propositions, should at least be free from the impact of affective commitments.

We must concede, I think, that there is value in this tradition. If we want to do history well, this approach seems one of the necessary components. As I have argued in this essay, we can properly share many of the scientific aspects of our work with our non-Christian colleagues. Where we should depart from this tradition is, I think, from the supposition that it is in itself a fully adequate way of knowing reality. Donald Mackay, the Christian philosopher of science, says this well concerning the claim of science generally to provide a "true" view of reality by looking at it objectively: "The truth is that it is the disappearance of man himself from the scientific picture that is illusory."[14] Detached objectivity is an illusion. It is a valuable illusion. For purposes of analysis, we must assume this stance—and in this age we simply must assume it if we are to be good historians. But we should not mistake it for a complete look at reality. Rather, we take this detached look at the picture only temporarily, knowing that ultimately we must deal with reality in its richer perspectives.

When we view reality in the perspective of this spiritual vision, not only are our perceptions of major patterns and relationships altered, but also our understanding becomes intimately bound up with the affective aspects of our knowing. When we see ourselves as frail creatures in a world of great spiritual forces and causes, our loves and commitments become central to our knowing. This affective knowledge is another way in which our Christianity can influence our academic work. The impulse of technological civilization is to view people as objects, consumers, numbers in a computer, abstract classes, as workers, industrialists, conservatives, radicals, and the like. The Christian on the other hand should insist that these abstract and scientific classifications of people are in a sense illusory, and that true knowledge of other persons must involve an affective dimension. We see persons as creatures of God, created in his image, to be valued individually. We attempt to value not only those like ourselves, and not only the rich and the powerful, but also the weak and the oppressed. We see God expressing himself in these creations, just as he does in the rest of nature, so that despite human sinfulness, our basic stance toward other persons and groups (even our enemies) should ultimately be affective—that of love.

Moreover, this affective stance that grows from viewing history and reality in the reorganized biblical and spiritual perspectives should add to our historical activity a prophetic dimension. I am not suggesting that we should be prophets instead of being historians; prophets too often do their history badly. Nonetheless, the affective dimensions of our knowing should impel us to see our task in exposing the false loves and affections, the idols and ideologies of our age. If we get glimpses of the spiritual dimensions of what we are doing, even the humble task of simply doing our job well takes on the significance of having some purpose in the cosmic spiritual struggles in which we participate.

Such a spiritual vision is a rich one compared to the arid moonscapes of the secular alternatives of our day. I see the difference in thinking back to the example with which I started. In the early 1970s, I again visited my graduate school friends. By then they had both left teaching history. The reason, it appears to me, is clear. LBJ and Vietnam ruined the hopes they had held out for the Democratic party. Seeing more clearly than historians usually do that history from a secular perspective has little other than immediate practical values, they got out. I am willing to insist that there must be other dimensions to reality that, given the eyes to see, we can see. Seeing such dimensions is valuable just in itself. It also is bound to affect, even if in many intangible ways, the whole course of what we do professionally.

5. History, Objectivity, and the Christian Scholar

M. HOWARD RIENSTRA

THE CLAIM that faith and history are compatible is not new or surprising. Many Christian historians have attempted to inspire and console each other with variations on this theme: faith in Jesus Christ is fully compatible with being a good historian. Good Christians can do good history. Of course, so can bad Christians—and non-Christians. And good Christians can also do bad history. But the point of the whole matter is that being a Christian in no way precludes one from being a good teacher and writer of history.

The claim is, however, deceptively simple and modest, because it allows for considerable ambiguity about the precise relationship that obtains between faith and history. To clarify this, I will caricature two extreme positions. The one position holds that an historian's devotion to Christ is personal and private and should rarely, if ever, influence the practice of being an historian. The compatibility of faith and history thus comes to mean little more than that they can be coincidentally present in one person. The Christian historian could be expected to have certain moral qualities that would affect his or her work, but such qualities would reside in good humanists or Marxists as well. Still, there would be little or no integration of faith and learning. The other position completely subordinates history to theology. It sees everything in history as an explicit showing of God's will and purposes, and of his judgments. History becomes theology teaching by example, and this position sees the task of the Christian historian as analogous to that of the writers of the Bible. The focal point of the study is God, not humans. History and homily become virtually indistinguishable. There is even a sociological correlate to these two positions. Those who hold to the first position tend to be found in public colleges and universities, while those who hold to the latter tend to be found in Bible colleges, seminaries, and denominational colleges. The former think the latter do bad history; the latter think the former have compromised their faith.

Part of the reason for this tension among Christian historians is that the historical profession in general is still committed to an idea of objectivity. Although objectivity has many meanings, it seems minimally to entail some kind of value-free inquiry. How can the Christian pretend to such an inquiry? The Christian's faith commitment is clearly value laden rather than value free. Since the Christian faith is often regarded as the clearest example of bias or prejudice, how then can the Christian historian conform in any way to the standard of objectivity? Each of the above extreme positions has a way of answering this question. The "private faith" contingent commit themselves to the possibility, at least, of methodological neutrality. They deny that their faith precludes objectivity, and they labor to exclude any implicit or explicit references to their faith in their work. They accept the positivist concept of history as a science. Their worship of God on Sunday and their witnessing to Christ on any day of the week are totally detached from their work as historians. The "history-as-theology" group choose rather to abandon objectivity and resort to subjectivity or relativism. They would reject the positivist assumption that neutrality and objectivity are possible. They would argue that all historians can be expected to do is be honest and explicit about their commitments. Some are equally frightened by the terms *subjectivity* and *relativism* and prefer to use the term *perspectivism.* Thus the Christian's perspective is as legitimate as any other perspective; and no history can be written apart from a perspective. Both of these positions are unsatisfactory.

Although good history is not necessarily to be identified with all kinds of objective history, there is no way to escape the problem that the idea of objectivity poses to the historian. Good history certainly entails being objective history in some sense. Occasionally, historians and philosophers argue about which discipline of the two has the greater attachment to the idea of objectivity. In fact, neither can avoid the idea. Even that grand cliché about writing history *wie es eigentlich gewesen ist,* which historians from Ranke on so naively asserted, means objectivity in some sense. Should all else fail, the difference between knowledge and ignorance rests upon the idea of objectivity, ". . . of things being the case whether people recognize them or not."[1] Some sense of objectivity is the only defense against complete subjectivity, or even worse, solipsism.

The major difficulty with the idea of objectivity is that it tends to become vacuous. Either it means too much or too little. Among historians, one view is represented by the positivists, who commit the so-called Baconian or inductivist fallacy.[2] They hold that historians should let the evidence or data speak for themselves. Not only should the historians' present commitments (religious, moral, political, or whatever) be systematically and rigorously excluded from the inquiry; but even their perceptions should be formally and mechanically ordered by a technique that will render impressions into knowledge without distortion of any sort. An opposite view is represented by idealists such as R. G. Collingwood and Benedetto Croce, for whom all history is the history of mind and thus contemporary to the historian. Objectivity means truth, and truth is coherence.[3]

John Passmore has written most persuasively on this problem of the vacuousness of the idea of objectivity. He has examined eight possible criteria for objectivity. The following three are illustrative:

> Criterion Two: An objective inquiry is one which begins from data which are literally such; i.e., which nakedly confront us.
>
> Criterion Six: An inquiry is objective only if it does not select from within its material.
>
> Criterion Eight: In objective inquiries, conclusions are reached which are universally acceptable.[4]

Most historians would immediately recognize that the discipline of history does not, and could not, conform to or satisfy these criteria. History, therefore, cannot pretend to be objective. Passmore's point is, however, that these criteria are too demanding and that no human inquiry, no science, could successfully satisfy them. Therefore, by the principle of nonvacuous contrast, one may not conclude that history cannot be objective unless one concludes, using these criteria, that objectivity in general is impossible. If there is no case in which anything is objective, then objectivity is a vacuous construct. The criteria for objectivity will have to be more modestly and reasonably constructed to preserve the idea.

One final dimension of the idea of objectivity must be noted for introductory purposes. This is again the problem of truth. Presuming that historians, like physicists, may make errors, the question remains, How would one know? How are fact and truth to be determined? Can we ever, even in principle if not in the practice of any inquiry, attain certainty? Israel Scheffler treats this problem as a dilemma between certainty and coherence:

> Either some of our beliefs must be transparently true of reality and beyond the scope of error and revision, or else we are free to choose any consistent set of beliefs whatever as our own, and to define "correctness" or "truth" accordingly. Either we suppose our beliefs to reflect the facts, in which case we beg the very question of truth and project our language gratuitously upon the world, or else we abandon altogether the intent to describe reality in which case our scientific efforts reduce to nothing more than a word game. We can, in sum, neither relate our beliefs to a reality beyond them, nor fail so to relate them.[5]

This is a dilemma of all science, of all theory. As an epistemological problem, it relates to the doing of history as well as to the doing of philosophy and science. It is a dilemma for Christians as well as for Marxists and humanists and all others.

As always, there is a temptation in the face of this dilemma to abandon objectivity in favor of skepticism or subjectivism. If Christian scholars presume to integrate their faith with their disciplinary inquiry, would that not in fact be a resort to subjectivism? Even the Christian doctrine of sin and the Fall have implications here. Do not Christians confess that even their understanding of God's revelation in creation, the Bible, and in Christ is distorted by sin in general, and by the peculiarities of their personal historical situation? Is not that a powerful argument for skepticism at least? And if, as we are increasingly told by both physicists and psychologists, even our perceptions are influenced by what we believe, should we not then abandon the idea of objectivity? Is not this especially true for Christians, whose beliefs are so explicit? The answer is, of course, no. Rather, the thesis of this article is, following Nicholas Wolterstorff, that some kind of objectivity must be retained in the Christian scholar's pursuit of knowledge. What Wolterstorff calls the "authentic Christian commitment"[6] of the Christian scholar is an essential and proper component of inquiry that does not compel resort to either skepticism or subjectivism. I will be arguing this thesis more fully below.

But first, we must turn to history more specifically. What is the nature of historical knowledge? It can be learned from the Greeks that it is a mode of inquiry. But it also comes from a Greek, Aristotle, that history is a comparatively insignificant mode of inquiry. Aristotle writes in the ninth chapter of the *Poetics:*

> Poetry is more philosophical and more weighty than history, for poetry speaks rather of the universal, history of the particular. By the universal I mean that such or such a kind of man will say or do such or such things from probability or necessity; that is the aim of poetry, adding proper names to the characters. By the particular I mean what Alcibiades did or what he suffered.[7]

History, for Aristotle, is clearly inferior to poetry and, *a fortiori*, to philosophy. Nor is this solely an ancient view of the matter. To many in the nineteenth century, history compared quite unfavorably to science. They saw science to be a nomothetic discipline, that is, given to the discovery of universal truths or laws. History, on the other hand, they saw to be idiographic, that is, given to statements about individuals or particulars. In the twentieth century the question has been raised whether historical explanation can even claim to be explanation. Since historical statements often do not even pretend to conform to the hypothetico-deductive (covering-law) model of explanation, some argue that they are not, therefore, explanations.[8] Thus caught between Aristotle in the ancient world and the positivists of the modern world, historians have chosen to grab both horns of the dilemma and to affirm that their discipline is both art and science. The historian's art is the art of storytelling, of narration; but his science is the methodological rigor of the examination of the evidence. To give the fullest possible account of something that happened is to explain what happened, and such explanation properly encompasses pattern, meaning, and wholeness, but not general laws. Historians seek a balance between art and science as the means to preserve, if not to re-establish, history's place in the academy.[9]

One further problem concerning the status of historical knowledge must be explored. Assuming that the historian can avoid the pitfalls of skepticism and subjectivism, what about relativism? What is the relationship between historical knowledge (about the past) and the whole complex of assumptions that characterize the thought world of the historian (the present)? Can the historian's analysis transcend in some way the limitations of the historian's present situation? Is there any way to avoid the consequences of what is known as the sociology of knowledge? In general, the answer is no. Such things as seeing, thinking, speaking, or writing are present activities even when about past things. Doing such present things does not allow for transcendence of present assumptions and commitments. But given this inability of historians to escape their own historicity, they still must be fair to the past. Good history requires such fairness. And good history entails objectivity. There must be a balance between known object (the past) and knowing subject (the present historian). The historian's role is to render the past intelligible to the present.

Achieving this balance is tricky. Some would allow the historian's present to weigh more heavily than would others. The following statement by Fritz Medicus illustrates such weighing toward the present:

> The partiality which is to be allowed him [the historian] is articulation into the spiritual movements of the time. . . . It must not express itself in judgments of value, but in the setting of questions by which the historian approaches the material of his research. It cannot injure the clarity of these problems if he takes a definite position in the spiritual movements of his own time.[10]

Medicus thinks that such articulation is consistent with objectivity. He is here anticipating two more recent trends in the doing of history: perspectivism and politicalization. We have already noted how some Christian historians have resorted to perspectivism in response to challenges from positivism. Perspectivism allows that every aspect of the historian's present is likely—and permissibly—to influence how he sees and reconstructs the past. Historical interpretation is necessarily the product of the historian's present perspectives. Medicus put it this way:

Every present allows a multitude of reconstructions of the past, each with a different perspective. Presentations of the same material can diverge without really contradicting one another; but they can even be mutually contradictory without one refuting the other.[11]

And all this still in favor of retaining some sense of objectivity! Political beliefs are, naturally, but one part of the spiritual movements to which the historian is to be articulated. Thus, varying political perspectives are not only acknowledged to exist, but they are positively encouraged. The most obvious examples of this recently have been the new left historians and the feminist historians. All are consistent with Medicus' idea of objectivity.

We must note, however, that this may also properly be called historical relativism, and that it becomes virtually indistinguishable, even descriptively, from subjectivism. If this is not subjectivism, then maybe that term too has become vacuous. There has been a noticeable shift of the balance between past and present toward the present. The present, the personal, and the parochial intrude despite the historian's desire to be fair to the past. Relativism in present circumstances means that one would read history only for its perspective. History is no longer good or bad, subjective or objective. Rather, one history would be distinguished from another primarily by the political, religious, or sexual preferences of its author. Having recently rejoiced at the demise of religiously, nationally, and racially prejudiced history, we now witness the rise of a politicized and perspectivized history that is equally bad.

Is there a way to restore some balance? Can the pitfalls of relativism and subjectivism be avoided? Do Christian historians want balance, or are they content with overt emphasis on their perspective?

One final, but equally futile, answer must be considered. Despite the initial enthusiasm, it is now clear that quantitative history is not the answer to relativism and subjectivism. There is nothing about quantitative techniques that guarantees good historical judgment. Historians employing quantitative methodology may be as prejudied, biased, or stupid as historians who do not. The controversy during the past decade surrounding the publication of *Time on the Cross* is a case in point. Charles Crowe's review of the controversy, in an article entitled "Slavery, Ideology and Cliometrics,"[12] is a devastatingly clear demonstration that neither prejudice nor stupidity can be avoided by using quantitative techniques. There is no simple answer to the problem of how to do good history. This is not, however, a counsel of despair, because there are some exciting developments within philosophy, particularly the philosophy of science, which Christian scholars should consider. Before answering the question of whether and how the Christian historian can avoid relativism and subjectivism, I will consider these recent developments.

Twentieth-century studies in the history and philosphy of science have had the important effect of challenging the presumed objectivity, neutrality, and finality of science and scientific theories. Science changes. Not only do hypotheses get discarded from time to time, but the very certainties of scientific law and theory are themselves subject to review and rejection. Is even the truth of science, then, relative? This question naturally arises out of the study of the history of science, but it has been given new impetus in this century by such diverse developments as Einstein's challenge to Newtonian theories, Pierre Duhem's rejection of the idea of a critical experiment, and the mathematician Henri Poincaré's seminal *Science and Hypotheses* (1902). These and other developments in philosophy were all brought together in the fifties and sixties by Thomas S. Kuhn. Kuhn's own studies in the Copernican revolution[13] were the foundation on which he constructed a view of scientific change in general. Traditional studies of the slow acceptance of Copernicanism had noted the impact of so-called nonscientific factors such as religion, simplicity, and even aesthetics. Kuhn has argued that such factors are not to be regarded as nonscientific, but rather that all such considerations are part of the paradigm in which all scientific activity and thought takes place.

Kuhn's *The Structure of Scientific Revolutions*[14] expressed this thesis about the paradigm. The paradigm consists of the total set of assumptions, beliefs, and commitments that prevail in a particular science and scientist at a particular time. The paradigm consists of such things as ideas about what constitutes real evidence, what procedures and methodologies are appropriate, and even ideas about regularity, uniformity, and aesthetic simplicity. Scientists may challenge, but never totally escape, the paradigm prevailing in their situation. The paradigm may even be such that it encourages scientists to think that their theories are finally and ultimately true. If some nineteenth- and early twentieth-century scientists did think that way, Kuhn would argue that the only remedy is a change in the paradigm. He proclaimed such a change in the twentieth century.

Kuhn argued that it is both necessary and proper for scientists to operate within the context of a paradigm. Others, however, would question whether it is proper that the paradigm contain even religious and irrational considerations. Kuhn would answer that even such assumptions as those about whether the world is a product of God's creative activity, and whether God's revelation is relevant to the doing of science, are part of the paradigm. Perhaps, Kuhn's opponents would argue, such matters have been part of past paradigms, but should they not be excluded from model paradigms? At this point, Kuhn's depen-

dence on Ludwig Wittgenstein becomes manifest. Following Wittgenstein, he argues that all such objections to irrational or religious factors
are purely arbitrary. They are arbitrary objections because all knowledge, all theory weighing, involves commitment or belief. Anyone who
pretends to know something with certainty is actually stating what he
believes to be true about something. There is, therefore, no grounds to
exclude one kind of commitment—namely religious—from science,
since all knowledge is based on commitment. Kuhn thus takes a position on both historical and epistemological grounds that holds traditional rationalism and empiricism to be inadequate accounts of how
scientists operate and how scientific change occurs.

Nicholas Wolterstorff has taken these developments in epistemology from Wittgenstein to Kuhn as dealing a deathblow to the theory of
truth which he calls foundationalism:

> Simply put, the goal of scientific endeavor, according to the foun-
> dationalist, is to form a body of theories from which all prejudice,
> bias, and unjustified conjecture have been eliminated. To attain
> this, we must begin with a firm foundation of certitude and build
> the house of theory on it by methods of whose reliability we are
> equally certain.[15]

The first sentence in this definition sounds like the traditional warnings
against subjectivism that are common to the literature about objectivity.
The second sentence, however, is crucial to Wolterstorff's meaning. He
expands that idea later: "In sum, the foundationalist sees the house of
genuine science as firmly based on a foundation of certitudes which
can be known non-inferentially."[16] Prescinding perversity or mental
incapacity, the foundationalist holds that people can discover some
truths that are objectively certain and unchanging. This, Wolterstorff
argues, is no longer a tenable assumption for any human science. As
far as the human enterprise of truth seeking is concerned, *veritas filia
temporis*.

Now while this may be slightly overstated, and while rationalists
and empiricists will insist that they have been prematurely buried, the
Christian scholar may be tempted to hope for too much. Is there
possibly an advantage that Christians may have in truth seeking, in
doing science? There are two ways that this question has been answered. Wolterstorff calls both of them "preconditionalism" because
they argue that the Christian's faith and acceptance of God's revelation
in both creation and the Bible establish the preconditions for the doing
of science. The more modest of the two ways simply argues that faith
precedes and makes knowledge possible. This seems compatible with
Kuhn's thesis that belief establishes the context in which science is
done. The less modest form of the thesis is that Christian faith can

save foundationalism and thus establish the immutable certainty of Christian science. Wolterstorff properly cautions against both, but he completely rejects the latter. The latter tends to confuse the inerrancy and immutability of God and his revelation with our errant and changing understanding of that revelation. Christian truth seeking is an activity that has a history just as non-Christian truth seeking does. Christian interpretations of history vary according to the time and place and circumstance of the historian almost as much as non-Christian interpretations of history do. The Christian scholar too must examine the whole range of beliefs that he brings to his scholarly activity. There is no royal—or easy—road for the Christian scholar.

There are several kinds of beliefs that constitute the paradigm of a particular science at a particular time. We analyze and choose theories consistent with such beliefs.[17] But the most important of such beliefs are those that Wolterstorff calls "control beliefs":

> We call these *control* beliefs. They include beliefs about the requisite logical or aesthetic structure of a theory, beliefs about the entities to whose existence a theory may correctly commit us, and the like. Because we hold them we are led to *reject* certain sorts of theories—some because they are inconsistent with those beliefs; others because though consistent with our control beliefs, they do not comport well with those beliefs.[18]

There are the commitments, religious as well as intellectual, that inform the thinking of all scholars, Christian and non-Christian. These control beliefs function to help us weigh theories. They are not a part of the theories being weighed, nor are they subject to theory-based analysis. They function pretheoretically even though under different circumstances they themselves may be weighed and rejected. But while we are doing a particular science, our control beliefs are an essential and proper element in choosing a theory on the basis of its consistency or comportment with those beliefs. Thus, in the doing of history our interpretation must be consistent with or comport well with the control beliefs of the Christian scholar.

At this point, Wolterstorff proposes a distinction that is essential to save Christian scholarship from charges of simple subjectivism or prejudice. This is the distinction between our "actual" Christian commitment and our "authentic" Christian commitment. Our "actual" Christian commitment consists of the totality of what we personally believe and do in our particular historical situation. It is a commitment to know and to do in response to Christ, but our knowing and doing is distorted by our finiteness as well as by our sin. Our knowing and doing is at best a fragmentary and imperfect obedience. This "actual" Christian commitment is limited by all such temporal and secular characteristics as our denominational affiliations, our citizenship, our social status, our education and the like. Our "actual" Christian commitment is an expression in thinking and doing of the particularities of our personal and historical situation.

Our "authentic" Christian commitment, on the other hand, must transcend in some way our "actual." It is rooted in the person of Jesus Christ and his revelation in creation and the Bible. It is an ideal type of some sort, but one that "ought" to be realized "actually." Our "authentic" Christian commitment may not be qualified by the distinctions that arise out of our personal and historical situation. Our "authentic" Christian commitment is based on the perfection of Christ and the truth of his Word. To him and his Word we are "authentically" committed. Such "authentic" Christian commitment is not reducible to any set of theological propositions, but such propositions would be properly incorporated within any actual coming-to-be of such a commitment.

There is, however, some ambiguity to the distinction between "actual" and "authentic" Christian commitment. Wolterstorff again:

> Authentic Christian commitment, as I have explained it, is relative to persons and to times. For authentic Christian commitment is how one's Christ-following *ought* to be actualized. And that varies not only from person to person, but also from time to time within a given person's life. . . . So authentic Christian commitment as a whole, but also the belief content thereof, is relative to persons and times.[19]

The difficulty here is that our "actual" Christian commitments are obviously relative to persons and times, but how can our "authentic" Christian commitment be relative without thereby becoming actual? Would that not be wholesale concession to relativism and all its horrors for Christians? I think that we can clarify the matter by substituting the word "related" for "relative" in the above quotation. Wolterstorff wishes to insist that our "authentic" commitment be related to our actual living and thinking. The "authentic" must not become merely an ideal type, an unrealizable standard of perfection. But it can be related without becoming relative. The belief content of our "authentic" commitment is to function as a control belief in our theory weighing. To do so, it must, paradoxically, become actual. The "authentic" must function as an *ought* in relation to the actual, but in what way?

At this point, Wolterstorff points out that there is a distinction between subjective and relative. He argues that while our "authentic" commitment may become relative, it must never be subjective. While agreeing that subjective is an inappropriate characteristic of theory weighing, I hold that relative is equally inappropriate. Perhaps the distinction between subjective and relative means more to a philosopher than it does to an historian, but I hope that the intent of the distinction is clear to both. The essential content of our "authentic" commitment is the unchanging Jesus Christ (Heb. 13:8); but our obedience is related to the peculiarities of our particular time and calling. The "authentic" is an *ought* that is relative only in the sense of being properly related to our particular time and place in the unfolding of God's plan. Thus our "authentic" commitment continues to transcend our "actual" commitments, however diligent may be our efforts to realize the normativeness of the "authentic" for "actual" Christian knowing and doing.

However, the paradox of trying to actualize the authentic is still a troublesome matter. The critical problem is to describe the belief content of both. The belief content of our "authentic" Christian commitment is that on which our "actual" commitment is based. We do not "actually" have it or know it for the simple reason that our having it or knowing it are part of our finite and sinful receiving of that content. But the real and objective content of our "authentic" commitment is Christ and his revelation in creation and the Bible, to which our "actual" must—in the sense of "ought" increasingly conform. It is the Christian scholar's "ought" to bring his science or his theory weighing into closer conformity to the truth of God in Christ and his revelation.

There still remain three ways of conceiving of the content of our "authentic" Christian commitment. The first is that the content is simply the person and work of Jesus Christ. However attractive this may be for confessing the basis of our salvation, it clearly is inadequate as a control belief in our theorizing. A second way is to think of it as a distillate out of the collective historical teaching and experience of all Christians. Christianity is nothing more or less than what Christians have thought, said, and done in all their diversity. Thus our "authentic" would be derived from "actual" Christian commitments with all of their shortcomings and inadequacies. But on what grounds would we think that accumulated, analyzed, or synthesized "actuals" could ever render something "authentic"? The "authentic" must be prior to and determinative of the "actual," not the other way around. One could arrive at a definition of some historic form of Christianity as a distillate out of other historic forms, but not the belief content of authentic Christian commitment.

Thus a third way is necessary. To help us to that third way, I should like to call attention to an analogous distinction used by the distinguished historian William J. Bouwsma. In an article on "Christian Adulthood," Bouwsma takes the task of writing an historical essay in the face of changing modes of Christian expression on the subject. Christians have thought differently, and sometimes confusedly, on what Christian adulthood is. The temptation to an historian would be to try to distill out of such changing historical expressions some kind of middle ground. Bouwsma avoids this, however, by formulating the following definition:

> I shall nevertheless try to show in this essay that Christianity does contain a characteristic conception of healthy human maturity, but to do so it will be necessary to distinguish between what I shall call historical and normative Christianity.[20]

Precisely! What is the normative idea that each historical idea is based on and rooted in? The normative cannot be distilled out of the mere historical. Rather, the historical is an expression of Christian efforts to realize the normative. This is what I see the distinction of Wolterstorff to mean. There is an authentic, that is, normative Christianity to which our actual, or historical, Christian commitment ought to conform.

What, then, is our authentic Christian commitment, our normative Christianity? Before answering, we must resist one final temptation. The question cannot be answered propositionally. That is, a proposition may refer to the content, but cannot itself contain the content. In other words, we cannot capture the essence of authentic Christianity in the words of a creed or a confession of faith—neither academic nor ecclesiastical. However important such creeds and confessions of faith may be, they are themselves finite constructions that are peculiar to the time and place of their authors. They are themselves actual and historical. Even Bouwsma's fine essay, which in my opinion states clearly the essence of authentic and normative Christian adulthood, is now a part of actual and historical Christianity, just as are the ideas of St. Augustine on the matter.

Now, finally, an answer: the belief content of our authentic Christian commitment is the revelation of God in creation and the Bible that we are privileged to know because of our living faith in Jesus Christ. In Christ we find our knowing and our doing to be in conformity and obedience to God's revelation. The truth of God's revelation, made open to people through Christ, is the belief content of our authentic Christian commitment.

How does this belief content of authentic Christian commitment function in the activities of the Christian scholar? Were one to be cute about the matter, one might answer: authentically and normatively. But I am now asking a question about actual and historical Christian scholars, and asking the question of how the authentic "ought" to function in their work. Wolterstorff, once again:

> As control, the belief-content of his authentic commitment ought to function both negatively and positively. Negatively, the Christian scholar ought to reject certain theories on the ground that they conflict or do not comport well with the belief-content of his authentic commitment. Positively, he ought to devise theories

which comport as well as possible with, or are at least consistent with, the belief-content of his authentic commitment.[21]

There is little more to say. What the Christian believes to be true, as he lives in Christ and receives God's revelation, is the basis of his theoretical or scientific activity.

But now this essay must return to the questions previously raised. May Christian scholars be seriously concerned to avoid the temptations of subjectivism and relativism in their several forms? And may Christian historians be seriously committed to objectivity in some sense as a necessary, although not sufficient, condition for the doing of good history? Yes, they must be so concerned and committed. The Christian who properly seeks wholeness and coherence in his believing, knowing, and doing cannot but be so concerned and so committed.

What, then, is an appropriate sense of objectivity? Given that the role of the historian is to render the past intelligible to the present, and that historians are professionally obliged to give accounts of the past that are both significant and truthful, how can objectivity be realized? And for the Christian historian there is the even more pressing problem of reconciling objectivity with religious commitment, both authentic and actual. To all of this, a deceptively simple possible solution has been suggested by Maurice Mandelbaum. He wrote:

> Our knowledge is objective if, and only if, it is the case that when two persons make contradictory statements concerning the same subject matter, at least one of them must be mistaken.[22]

Historical accounts are subject to the principle of contradiction. Two contradictory accounts of the past cannot both be true; one or both must be mistaken or false.

Such a modest and limited sense of objectivity is appealing to historians, and rather obviously not vacuous. But how, given this limited sense of objectivity, are mistakes to be determined? Historians can and do make all sorts of mistakes, but in this context the critically relevant concern is with the handling of evidence. How historians use the evidence of the past that is available to them is basic to all such modest claims to objectivity. The available evidence establishes the limiting conditions for historical accounts. They must be faithful to that evidence. The critical analysis and interpretation of all available evidence is crucial to the determination of the truth or falsehood of historical accounts. Regardless of the sexual, political, economic, or religious commitments of the historian, the account must conform with a reasonable analysis of the evidence. If not, one, or both, or all accounts may be mistaken.

The historian's pretheoretical and theoretical commitments are, as I have argued above, essential and inescapable components of truth seeking. They do not necessarily produce contradictory accounts of the same subject matter. Rather, such commitments, including religious commitments, will most likely lead to complementary accounts in which the above standard for objectivity is preserved. Does the belief content of the Christian scholar's commitment allow for this?

The thesis of this essay suggests an affirmative answer, but I must acknowledge difficulties. The proper use of religious commitment in scholarship should not be construed as allowing for, if not encouraging, the writing of parochial or sectarian history. There is no need to return to the controversies between, for example, Protestant and Catholic historiography. The Christian scholar cannot affirm objectivity by merely allowing one's "actual" Christian commitment to mold one's scholarship. Rather, the scholarly ideal for the Christian historian is that the historical account is consistent with and comports well with the "authentic" control beliefs of Christianity. All is to be brought into obedience and conformity to the timeless Christ and his revelation. The non-Christian scholar has parallel and similar religious commitments that comport well with his truth seeking and quest for objectivity. Christians do not claim exclusively to be objective or to be better truth seekers than their non-Christian colleagues. But neither do they accept any lesser status than do their non-Christian fellow scholars. The "authentic" religious commitments of the Christian scholar are fully compatible with the modest and nonvacuous criteria of objectivity presented above. The Christian should be content with nothing less.

6. Christian Faith and Historical Method: Contradicition, Compromise, or Tension?

Robert T. Handy

THE CENTURIES-old debate about how faith and reason are to be related has been and continues to be carried on in many forms. Certain classic positions on the issue have long been stated and defended, yet the debate sporadically breaks out afresh. One of the points at which the problem repeatedly arises is reflected in the first part of the title of this essay: "Christian faith and historical method." The two things are so different that it may seem anomalous to bring them together; for the one is a major historical faith, the other a particular scholarly method. Yet both the faith and the method have long histories, and these histories have become intertwined so that many persons have found that they have to come to terms with both and with the relationship between them, as vastly different as they are.

On the one hand, Christian faith has shown itself to be one of the great historic faiths of the world, exhibiting its power in human life as it has oriented the lives of millions of persons to God as made known in Jesus Christ, given them a view of the world as existing under divine providence, steeped them in Scripture as the authoritative guide to the living of life and the making of decisions, and gathered them into communities of faith in which lives of worship and service have been nurtured. The faithful are encouraged to love God with heart, soul, strength, and mind; they are led to see meaning and purpose in life, and they are provided with certain insights about past, present, and future. The resources of faith bring solace in times of grief and encouragement in dealing with life's crises. Christian faith has been presented in very many styles and forms in past and present; its institutional forms are highly varied and complex.

On the other hand, historical method also has a long history. Though its beginnings can be traced back to ancient times, it was developed and systematized during the periods we typify as the Renaissance, the Enlightenment, and the modern Age of Science. The method has been patiently developed into a rather keen-edged instrument as it guides its users to collect data from the past, to criticize and test those materials for authenticity and to determine their original meaning, and then to interpret them so that we may better know how

84 ROBERT T. HANDY

the present came to be out of the past. As Albert C. Outler has summed up a complex matter cogently, "The historian's chief business, we might perhaps agree, is the re-collection and re-presentation of selected segments of the human past *in an intelligible narration based on public data verified by scientific observation.*"[1] The historical method is thus quite limited and precise: it deals with observable data in a critical way, and it puts its users on guard against their own biases and subjectivities, insisting that their conclusions be submitted for scrutiny by others.

The method has been developed over many centuries, but much of its development came during that period in Western history that we label the Enlightenment, and under Enlightenment auspices primarily. But Enlightenment faith and Christian faith have not infrequently moved in quite different directions. The historian Crane Brinton once remarked that "the basic structure of Christian belief survived, . . . not without heresies and schisms, until, roughly, the late seventeenth century when there arose in our society what seems to me clearly to be a new religion, certainly related to, descended from, and by many reconciled with, Christianity. I call this religion simply Enlightenment, with a capital E."[2] Brinton carefully notes that this new religion was reconciled by many with Christianity, but it was new, and as time wore on its differences with Christian faith became clearer—especially on the critical point of the nature of reason. Friedrich Heinrich Jacobi spoke for many tortured people early in the nineteenth century when he wrote: "I . . . am a heathen in my reason and a Christian with my whole heart; I swim between two bodies of water which will not unite so that together they can hold me up, but while the one continuously holds me, the other is constantly letting me sink."[3]

The gulf was further widened by the spread of scientism and naturalism in the nineteenth century. To summarize briefly a long story as told, for example, by Van A. Harvey in his book *The Historian and the Believer,* by the dawn of the twentieth century it was perceived that the new methods of historical study expressed a new morality of historical judgment, one that celebrates methodological skepticism and that proceeds by raising doubts at every juncture. This new morality of historical judgment is quite different from the old ethic so long nurtured within Christianity, which celebrated faith and belief and regarded doubt as sin.[4] Small wonder that some were troubled by the spread of historical method, for it seemed to be bringing the camel's nose of an alien position within the tent of faith.

Against this background one can understand those who declared at the opening of the present century that between Christian faith and historical method in the way it had been developed there could only be contradiction and opposition. This was expressed in both Catholic and Protestant circles, in the suppression of Modernism in the former and in the emergence of Fundamentalism in the latter. Sometimes it was the Christian church historians, such as Arthur C. McGiffert and Henry P. Smith, who employed the critical method as they studied the households of faith, who fell under attack as trying to reconcile the irreconcilable, and of evading the contradictions between the faith and the method of critical history. One of that company was Walter Rauschenbusch, the Rochester church historian who in 1907 published the seminal work in the history of the social gospel, *Christianity and the Social Crisis.* In a slashing pamphlet on the book, Dr. I. M. Haldeman observed that its primary problem was that it was a product of church history, and that "church history is, and always must be, a peril to the student for the ministry."[5] A peril, indeed, for any Christian believer, for the method requires one to be critical of his own position. The dilemma was never more poignantly stated than by Ernst Troeltsch, who in 1923 explained to an Oxford audience that his quest for a vital and effective religious position had led him into a passionate interest in theology and philosophy. "I soon discovered, however," he exclaimed, "that the historical studies which had so largely formed me, and the theology and philosophy in which I was not immersed, stood in sharp opposition, indeed even in conflict, with one another."[6]

While some believers thus see contradiction and opposition between Christian faith and historical method with all that that implies, others find themselves uncomfortably caught between them and feel driven to make some compromise. They are persons of faith, but they are also children of the Enlightenment and of the modern world, and they have been strongly influenced by the values of the historical method. Somewhat pragmatically, they live in both worlds. An example of the pattern of compromise was given by Shailer Mathews, long-time professor of historical theology and dean of the Divinity School of the University of Chicago. He declared that he was a Modernist Christian as he spoke for many like himself in the early part of the present century. He insisted that he and those like him both historically and by preference took as their starting point "the inherited orthodoxy of a continuing community of Christians"; and he spoke warmly of that stance, saying that "the place of evangelical Christianity in social and ethical life, the aid it gives to millions of human hearts, the moral impetus it has given social reforms, forbid treating Christianity as an unborn child of human thought." But for him the Modernist was critic and historian before being a theologian, one who "may be said to be first of all a Christian who implicity trusts the historical method of an approach to Christian truth." Hence he arrived at his oft-quoted definition of Modernism as "*the use of the methods of modern science to find, state and use the permanent and central values of inherited orthodoxy in meeting the needs of a modern world,*"[7] a position that has seemed to many to leave the scientific method as the real authority in matters of faith. To many critics this seemed to be capitulation to the modern world view; to others who found it a useful and even necessary coming to terms with the modern world, it still seemed to be something of a compromise, an effort to serve two masters.

In my own personal struggle with the problem of faith and historical method, I find myself returning again and again to the concept of tension. In fulfilling my vocation as a Christian historian— and one who works by choice primarily as a narrative historian of the church—I have taken faith as my point of departure. Much of my understanding of the church comes from biblical and theological sources, from faith. I have come to believe that the Christian church is a divine/human reality, one of divine intention and of human response. But whatever else it is, it is a human institution, subject to the winds of change and the pressures of history, an institution with a temporal history that is complex and varied. Indeed, as convinced a believer in the divine origins of the church as Karl Barth observed that "the being of the community in its temporal character is hidden under considerable and very powerful appearances to the contrary."[8] A church historian as believer can theologize about the church and can point to its hidden character, but as an historical scholar making use of a tested method, the church historian—like any historian—should stick to the observable data and cite the concrete evidence in narration, analysis, and interpretation. This is not to say that the concrete data may not be handled in a lively way. Owen Chadwick's advice here is pointed: "To be a historian, you need, first evidence, and second evidence. But you also need imagination; not imagination which dreams dreams, or feigns fantasies, but imagination which can clothe the dry statistic in the document, and turn it from flatness to life."[9]

That is easier to say than to do, but it does point to the importance of a disciplined imagination in the doing of history. The discipline is provided by historical method, which is not to say that other methods of studying the church or the world are not proper and valid; but the historian's task is a specialized and defined one. Indeed, that task when well done may be quite useful to other approaches, especially when the historian sticks to what the method can help him or her do best. In the preface to his excellent book *Tradition and the Modern Word*, Brian A. Gerrish confesses that beneath his role as historian there lurks a theologian, but that he has deliberately—for the time being at least— focused on the historical task. He explains that "my modus operandi has become historical even though my final designs have never ceased to be systematic; and I hold the view that history is of no use to the theologian unless it is permitted to follow its own rules, however inconvenient they may prove to be."[10] I suspect that there lurks a theologian and/or a philosopher in most historians; the better they are aware of that and yet remain faithful to historical method, however inconvenient, the better and more acceptable historical work they will do.

The words "however inconvenient" suggest that there will always be tension between Christian faith and historical method, between the believer and the historian, and inside the believer who is a historian or who uses the historical method as part of the day's job. But the tension can be creative and not destructive, for within the faith itself are emphases that call some of us to do critical historical work and help all of us to see real values in the method. Certain aspects of various Christian doctrines not only permit us but encourage us to take history with full seriousness and to use critical historical methods wholeheartedly.

For example, a basic Christian doctrine is that God created this world and sustains it in time. Therefore, to learn as much as we can about the creation and the creatures is also to learn more about the Creator. H. Richard Niebuhr once put it thoughtfully this way: "Hence any failure of Christians to develop a scientific knowledge of the world is not an indication of their loyalty to the revealed God but to their unbelief. . . . Resistance to new knowledge about our earthly home and the journey of life is never an indication of faith in the revealed God but almost always an indication that our sense of life's worth rests on the uncertain foundations of our confidence in humanity, our society, or some other evanescent idol."[11] The knowledge that comes through the application of historical method may be inconvenient and even painful, but to resist it or turn from it may give evidence of our lack of faith; for an unblinking facing of the reality that is disclosed by this method—and it is only one of the ways to face reality, but an important one—may help us to learn more about the ways of the Creator, the creation, and the creatures.

The doctrine of incarnation is another central one, developed in somewhat different ways by various Christian traditions. An important aspect of most discussions of the incarnation of God in Christ emphasizes that the Eternal takes human life so seriously that God sent his Son into the world to live in the flesh among humans, sharing our burdens. As the second letter to the Corinthians puts it, God was in Christ reconciling the world to himself; through Christ, God entrusted the message of reconciliation to human beings, thus taking our history seriously.[12] In discussing the Christian doctrine of incarnation, New Testament scholar Sir Edwyn Hoskyns has declared: "In consequence the Christian religion is not merely open to historical investigation, but demands it, and its piety depends upon it."[13] So we are to take our history seriously, seeking to understand it by whatever available methods and instruments are at hand. Whatever we can learn about the forces in human history that tend to enrich and liberate human life can be a service to all persons of good will; conversely, it is important to know about those factors in history that tend to degrade and oppress human life so that we can be on guard against them. Insofar as scientific historical method can help to clarify for us the forces that make for the ennoblement or the destruction of human life, Christians can and should employ it in their efforts to serve God and humankind.

Some of the most intense theological debates in history have revolved around the nature of human sinfulness. Some have minimized it, while others, such as Jonathan Edwards and Reinhold Niebuhr in North American theological history, have emphasized it, on the basis of their study of Scripture and theology and of their observations of the human past and present. These and many others have illustrated with compelling power the tendency of us who are finite creatures to throw up a smoke screen of rationalization around ourselves to hide our self-centeredness and sinfulness from ourselves and from others. We are continually trying to rewrite the story of the past, even—or perhaps especially—the story of our own past to serve our particular purposes, often very partisan indeed. We in the churches may often be trying to revise the past to suit our present needs and to support plans of our own, though those plans may be quite ambivalent, to put it mildly, with respect to the purposes of the Eternal.

Whatever the limitations of the historical method, and they are many, it has its utilities in enabling us and others to penetrate through those smoke screens of rationalization, through those distortions we so easily create as we look back on the past, indeed often constructing one that never was. The use of historical method can help to keep us honest; it can help to protect us against our inclination to distort both past and present; it can assist us to guard against the temptation to intellectual sin and pride; it can aid us in keeping our own positions under judgment and thus open to further light that may come from the study of Scripture and of history. The method of critical history can even help us learn about and from our enemies, which may be a very important first step in loving them—which the Christian is commanded to do. With his customary and eminently quotable clarity, Richard Niebuhr once declared that "critical history is for societies the great psychiatric process by which they reconstruct their past—not according to their wishes but in accordance with a surer understanding of what happened to them and what they did, than their uncriticized, emotion-laden, mythical, and legendary memories allow."[14] The historical method can thus be a very apt instrument in helping us understand the Christian doctrine of sin and in guarding us against our tendencies to cast ourselves and our pasts in more favorable light than the facts permit. And conversely, it can keep us from putting down unfairly the views, theologies, and deeds of others with whom we happen to disagree.

In suggesting that reflection on such doctrines as creation, incarnation, and sin does provide legitimation for the use of historical method, I am, of course, pointing to secondary though, I think, important aspects of or inferences from those doctrines. Unquestionably, the use of critical historical method is tension-creating, for it raises difficult questions, operates as a check on unthinking enthusiasm and undisciplined imagination, and reminds us of unpleasant chapters in the history of the church that we may wish were not there. Having arisen only in part from Christian sources and influences, the historical method is perhaps always something of a naturalized outsider within the tradition, and is in some tension with it. But properly understood, that tension can be a creative one as it helps us to see ourselves as others see us, and aids us in understanding our own limitations and those of our predecessors in the faith. At the same time, it can assist us in seeing steadily and more accurately the achievements of Christians and churches in history, to appreciate moments of insight and courage in clear perspective and not through too romanticized a haze, and to glimpse in a relatively unclouded way many of the treasures of Christian spirituality. It can help us see the history of other religions in fair perspective, understanding them more for what they were and are in their strengths and limitations, rather than seeing them only as they appeared to be to various Christian observers through the centuries—though that witness is part of the story too. But all this does involve tension within us and among us as we see the gaps between the ideal and the real, between romantic memory and reinterpreted reality, between fancy and fact. If we are unwilling to face this tension, I think we testify more to our unfaith than to our faith. There are certainly many other tasks of reflection and scholarship for Christians to do, but the use of historical method is often helpful, not only for the person who makes history a vocation or avocation, but also for those whose talents lie primarily in other directions.

Part of the reason that historical method has created tension within the faith and among the faithful is because some have used it as their primary approach to a philosophical or theological position. The historical method has been developed out of many sources, and as a method, as I have argued here, it can be used wholeheartedly by the Christian, in full awareness of the tensions it can cause. It can be helpful in discerning things about the world, the faith, and the church that cannot be found in other ways; but as a method it does not alone provide an adequate ground for a philosophy or a theology. It may be a helpful corrective but is hardly an adequate source for a full interpretation of life. Sir Herbert Butterfield has long been a teacher of and example for Christian historians, and his words, though familiar, are worth emphasizing in this connection:

> I am unable to see how a man can find the hand of God in secular history, unless he has first found that he has an assurance of it in his personal experience. If it is objected that God is revealed in history through Christ, I cannot think that this can be true for the mere external observer, who puts on the thinking-cap of the ordinary historical student. It only becomes effective for those who have carried the narrative to intimate regions inside themselves, where certain of the issues are brought home to human beings. In this sense our interpretation of the human drama rests finally on our interpretation of our most private interpretation of life, and stands merely an extension to it.[15]

Or as it is so often less elegantly put, historical interpretations and judgments are influenced by one's value system, which in part, at least, is shaped by whatever faith or faiths, avowed or unavowed, one holds. David L. Schindler has recently stated the point in a somewhat paradoxical way that I find helpful. Indicating that he does not wish "to negate the critical forces set in motion by the Enlightenment nor to deny contemporary history," he declares that "Christian thinkers can take history seriously only by affirming that reality is not simply historical, that being is not identical to history."[16] What such a stance does is highlight what historical method really is, as a limited one that can be put to use by those of various faiths and philosophies. Indeed, it can help to mediate between them, because it can help us all to understand ourselves and others better. In the long run, this may reduce tensions within faiths and between them; in the short run, it is likely to increase them, for when you use the channels of historical investigation to look at your own and others' views and deeds, you expose your own position to the challenges and criticisms of others. But the faith that cannot stand the risk of such testing is hardly adequate for the living of life, and can hardly be in God as the Creator and Sustainer who is disclosed in the sources of Christian faith.

In conclusion, I want to speak out of my own experience as a Christian who employs the historical method as honestly as he can within certain specified areas and in a particular way. I have found my own calling primarily as a church historian, rather than as one who delves directly into such fields as political, social, or intellectual history, though I admire those who work effectively in such fields, and I depend on their work. At the same time, I find myself drawn to the task of writing narrative history, of telling and retelling the story of important chapters in the history of the church, while recognizing that there is an analytical aspect to any effort of historical interpretation. I applaud a comment made by Edwin Van Kley, who explained: "I for one still have immense sympathy for the notion that history is to serve present society as its cultural memory and that this can best be achieved by carefully reconstructing past epochs and events in their full variety and complexity, by artistically telling the stories, and by writing it all in ordinary, jargon-free language for the general reading public."[17] The narrative church historian strives to communicate what has been learned out of the study of the complex history of the church in story form, trying to make alive again the thoughts and deeds of those who went before this generation but who contributed so much to what our generation thinks, feels, and has by way of literary and institutional resources. The task calls for one to be critical, to note where wrong turns may have been made, where faith seems to have been compromised too readily to cultural conventions or pressures, where the being of the church in its temporal character was deeply hidden under considerable and very powerful appearances to the contrary. But it also calls for telling what was accomplished, how persons found direction and purpose for their lives, how the quality of human life was lifted, how sacrifices were made, and how illuminating and inspiring words were spoken and written. The historical method is an indispensable ally in all this; to try to do the task without it would be to deprive ourselves of an important resource. To be sure, the use of the method in seeking evidence and clarifying facts and interpretations is only one of the things that Christians are to be about. But Van Harvey made an important observation when he said, "A fact cannot provide the ground or the object of faith when faith is properly understood, although it can awaken faith and provide the symbols that faith uses."[18] Christian faith and historical method are quite different realities indeed, but the faithful can make use of the method, for the tensions that arise can be creative, and the method can play a role in the clarification of faith.

7. Social Science History: An Appreciative Critique

ROBERT P. SWIERENGA

IN THE 1950s a "paradigm revolution" (in the Kuhnian sense[1]) began in the discipline of history that challenged traditional historical scholarship as it had been practiced for generations. The revolution began with the cliometricians in economic history and then spread to the political behavioralists and social historians.[2] By the 1970s the movement had matured, and in 1974 the advocates of the "new history," as it was called,[3] forged an interdisciplinary alliance—the Social Science History Association—with historically inclined scholars in the sister disciplines, in order to enhance the methodological and theoretical tools in the historian's handbag. This organization and its journal *Social Science History* (1976–), together with other new specialized journals, associations, and supporting networks, soon expanded into fresh fields—historical demography, family history, childhood and aging, social deviance, ethnic history, peasant studies, psychohistory, urban history, and rural history, to name a few.[4]

Before describing the meaning and purposes of the new history, I must clarify its various aspects. One can distinguish three categories or levels, each narrower than the other: social scientific history, quantification, and computer-aided (or computerized) history. The broadest term, social scientific history, is history that is theoretical, collective, and comparative.[5] Explicit statements of concepts, hypotheses, or models in the social sciences give direction and focus to the work. The research process involves the systematic accumulation of more or less uniform individual observations, which are aggregated or grouped, and compared systematically over time, or between spatial units, or among subgroups.

At the second level is quantification, or "historiometry," to use an old term of Frederick Adams Woods,[6] or "quanto-history," which is Jacques Barzun's more recent pejorative label.[7] Quantitative history is a blending of numbers and history, the reliance on numerical rather than verbal symbols, and the use of standard social statistics to measure the significance of relationships between attributes of persons or groups. Finally, at the lowest definitional level is computer-aided history, which simply means that a data base is converted into machine-readable form and then combined, tallied, or otherwise "crunched" by a computer. Computer processing time is measured in nanoseconds (a billionth of a second), but the procedure is otherwise little different in results from former hand-tabulation methods. For most historian users, a computer is merely a super calculator, not a living, silicon-chip miracle "brain" that can surpass human intelligence, as a 1978 *Time* essay predicted.[8]

The new history is not so new. Actually, it is part of an old tradition in the discipline. Frederick Jackson Turner's seminars at the turn of the century included primitive social science techniques and an emphasis on environmental forces that shaped human behavior.[9] In 1904, Turner summarized his views: "No satisfying understanding of the evolution of this American people is possible without calling into cooperation many sciences and methods hitherto little used by the American historian. . . . The method of the statistician as well as of the critic of evidence is absolutely essential."[10]

Despite Turner's admonition, American historians remained primarily committed to the Rankean tradition of value-free, factual narration. History clearly stood apart from the nascent social sciences—which had become increasingly ahistorical—until about 1930, when European scholars, notably the French *annales* school, espoused social scientific methods and theories.[11] A few American historians subsequently adopted the new thinking in the 1950s. Samuel P. Hays, a master teacher and conceptualizer, in an address to secondary school teachers in 1959, offered the first popularized rationale for social scientific history. In his lecture "History as Human Behavior," Hays urged teachers to revitalize their courses by focusing on "the human side of the past" rather than on formal institutions and "presidential history." The systematic study of "human experience and behavior," Hays declared, would render "solid and concrete generalizations . . . regarding past human experience."[12] Hays devoted the remainder of his influential career to fleshing out these seminal ideas, which he called a "behavioral approach" to history.[13]

Hays's colleagues at the University of Iowa, William O. Aydelotte and Allan G. Bogue, shared his vision and were busily engaged in behavioral studies of British members of parliament and American farmers and congressmen, respectively.[14] After working for some years with statistical methods and then with computers, Aydelotte developed a reasoned, theoretical defense of social scientific methods that was published as the lead article in the *American Historical Review* in 1964.[15] Despite its irenic tone, this statement is intellectually robust and has become a classic defense of quantitative methods. The principal value of quantification, said Aydelotte, is that it provides a means of verifying generalizations that are "implicitly quantitative in character." In addition, the use of numerical data provides for greater accuracy, speed, and objectivity. It also "offers a systematic means of testing hypotheses" and may open up new lines of inquiry. Contrary to what critics had charged, Aydelotte patiently explained; "No one well versed in this line of work would argue that all historical materials can be quantified, that the figures provide any final demonstration of the broader inferences derived from them, or that the figures tell the whole story." Quantification, for Aydelotte, has a limited role. It is "merely an ancillary tool," although "a tool of exceptional power." But its use does not involve "a change of the fundamental objectives of historical research."[16]

While the Iowa triumvirate were clarifying their ideas and honing their skills, Lee Benson was gaining notoriety as an ardent advocate of social scientific history. In the mid-1950s, Benson obtained a post-doctoral fellowship to study with Paul Lazarsfeld and Seymour Martin Lipset at Columbia University. Benson's lengthy report on his work, "Research Problems in American Political History" (1957), became the agenda for the new political historians.[17] It is laden with social science terms and concepts—"objective data," "potentially verifiable hypotheses," "systematic methods"—but the key phrase is a pithy five-word question: "Who voted for whom, when?"[18] This simple statement of who did what when (rather than what A said to B or thought about C) changed the direction of American historiography. It prompted the creation of the vast historical data archive at the Inter-University Consortium for Political Research in Ann Arbor; it spawned dozens of dissertations and books; and eventually this perception produced the Social Science History Association.[19]

No one is more insistent on the need for a "genuinely scientific historiography" than is Benson. For two decades he has urged historians, especially younger scholars, to use explicit theory, social science methods, numerical data, and whenever possible computer-processing, in order to fulfill their main task—to develop general laws of human behavior. Like the English historian Henry T. Buckle, Benson's counterpart of a century ago, Benson insists that past human behavior can be studied scientifically, provided that scholars create and fully utilize huge machine-readable data archives. If historians follow this cooperative, sharply focused agenda and develop powerful theories, Benson argued in 1966, then "the prediction does not seem absurd that two decades from now, say by 1984 [sic], a significant proportion of American historians will have accepted Buckle's two basic presuppositions: (1) past human behavior can be studied scientifically; (2) the main business of historians is to participate in the overall scholarly enterprise of discovering and developing general laws of human behavior."[20] In short, unlike Aydelotte, a so-called "soft quantifier," Benson is a "hard quantifier" who desires a "deliberative societal history."[21]

The reaction to Benson's hypotheses was strong. Many historians believed that he and his colleagues were ideologues and not historians.[22] The dividing line between a behavioral *approach* and behavior-al*ism* is admittedly a thin one, and practitioners sometimes cross the line unawares and make an ideology of a method. Nevertheless, few social scientists and *no* historians that I know subscribe to a simple stimulus-response model of behavior. Most are willing to consider the inner structure of behavior, and to include ideas and feelings in their analyses. But historians emphasize behavior because they can usually *document* this by direct observation or from surviving evidence, whereas they must *infer* what individuals or groups felt or thought. Sometimes, of course, historians must infer behavior of past persons, as when they use indirect evidence or deduce individual behavior from aggregate data. But in such cases there are statistical tests to help ferret out bias and incorrect inferences. For these and other reasons, behavioral historians de-emphasize literary sources and concentrate instead on "ecological" variables, such as age, sex, family, education, ethnicity, religion, occupation, wealth, and the like.

Some scholars believe that there is a fundamental gulf between history as one of the humanities and as a behavioral science. Robert Zemsky stated the proposition starkly: "Whenever a historian embarks on a statistical analysis he crosses a kind of personal Rubicon."[23] Sheldon Hackney, in his article "Power to the Computers: A Revolution in History?" asserted bluntly that computer-assisted research methods inevitably lead historians toward the social sciences.[24] Other scholars disagree with the necessity argument, believing that one can use scientific methods and theories without seeking ultimate truth or answers to the moral questions perplexing society.[25] Whether one personally "crosses the Rubicon" or not, the behavioral revolution has been fundamental. And something larger is at issue than mere methodology or a technical reorientation. Simply reaffirming the scientific method, after all, would hardly have stirred up the emotional reaction and the turmoil concerning mission that occurred in the 1960s. Rather, social scientists have experienced a profound transformation in which assumptions about human nature, social processes, and the scientific enterprise have changed.[26]

The key articles of faith for behavioral historians include the principles of regularity or predictability, probability, testability, falsability, and objectivity.[27] Behavioralists recognize that no two people are alike and that people are unpredictable; but they also insist that human behavior in a given society is socially determined and quite uniform. Christians also know that there is order and pattern in human behavior because God is the creator and sustainer of an orderly universe. Even unpredictable actions of individuals create a regular pattern in the aggregate. These regularities are not only discernible, but they can be expressed in theories that have explanatory or predictive power. Such

theoretical statements, Paul Lazarsfeld has noted, "will always be prob-
abilistic ones, . . . [because] probability ideas play a dominant role,
explicitly or implicitly, in the study of human behavior."[28] Thus historians must forego the quest for definitive answers about the past and
recognize, in Aydelotte's words, that "estimates of probability are the
one kind of fairly reliable knowledge that they may expect to get."[29]
Third, behavioralists begin with theoretical formulations or hypotheses
that are testable and definitions that are operational. As Hanz Eulau
said: "No matter how concrete or abstract conceptually, [definitions]
must be relevant empirically."[30] What cannot be tested with hard data
cannot be analyzed.

A fourth principle of behavioralists is falsability and its corollary,
tentativeness. It is assumed that absolute verification is impossible in
scientific enterprise: scientific knowledge can only be tentative; truths
are temporary until disproved. Thus, behavioralists prefer to verify
hypotheses by the process of negation. In social statistics, a relationship
is significant if one cannot reject the null hypothesis (that is, that no
statistically significant relationship exists). If a scientific theory cannot
be absolutely verified, however, because of the limits of data and
method, neither for the same reason can it be decisively falsified.[31]
Nevertheless, social scientists find it more satisfying intellectually to
attempt, in Eulau's words, to "reduce ignorance" than to "create knowledge."[32] They also readily acknowledge the tentativeness of their findings, and subject themselves to critical peer scrutiny through the process
of publishing their research results in refereed journals and mono-
graphs. This process of scholarly review and sometimes of replication
by others of one's research procedure encourages scientists to be more
objective in their research design and data analysis. Social scientific
scholars also increase objectivity by relying on time-tested, standardized
techniques of sampling, statistical analysis, and data description. The
realm of objectivity, of course, is confined to the collection and analysis
of data, not the selection of the research questions and the explanation
or interpretation of the findings. These crucial stages of scientific
research are clearly subjective, and claims to the contrary are mis-
guided.

The behavioral approach, then, is based on a sophisticated and
vigorous empiricism—one that closely intertwines social science theory
with a verification process based on hard data. Theory and research
are linked in a symbiotic relationship. Research untutored by theory
may prove trivial, and theory without solid evidence may be specious.

Having stated the credo of behavioralists, I will briefly contrast
this with the traditional humanistic approach to historical studies. The
contrast, it should be noted, is mainly a heuristic device, because in
practice it is not always possible to draw clear lines between social

scientists and humanists. First, humanist historians concentrate on the unique situation of a given time and place rather than on the uniformities that transcend that time and place. Daniel Boorstin, Director of the Library of Congress and historian of the United States, describes the traditional role of the historian as being the "high priest of uniqueness": "If the historian has any function in the present welter of the social scientific world," Boorstin insists, "it is to note the rich particularity of experience, to search for the piquant aroma of life. As contrasted with the abstract, antiseptic dullness of numbers, 'cases,' and prototypes, the historian as humanist is a votary of the unrepeatability of all experience, as well as of the universal significance of each human life."[33]

Second, the humanist historian rejects all set methods and theories. The concern is the subject, the story itself, and the method is intuitive and synthetic.[34] One explains by describing. Third, the story should be written for the general public and be told in elegant literary style, with subtlety and finesse. Social scientists lack "a mastery of their native tongue," charges Jack H. Hexter. They write "dull history," and dull history is "bad history," read only by fellow specialists.[35] A fourth difference is source material. Humanists seek literary accounts—newspapers, private manuscripts, government testimony and reports, and the like—which contain thoughts but seldom describe behavior in a systematic way. Behavioral historians also consult literary sources, but they concentrate on serial records—voting lists, election polls, census reports, tax records, emigration lists, and so forth, all of which contain empirical data.

These two contrasting approaches to the historian's task appear to be at opposite poles of the methodology spectrum. But is the spectrum a continuum with many gradations, or is it bi-polar, with nodules clustered at each end? The answer to this question is largely existential and hinges on the psychological make-up, feelings, and experiences of individual scholars. The discipline of history is in a state of virtual anarchy today. Professor Aydelotte's aphorism has become a classic: "History is what historians do." Not only is "everyman his own historian" (to paraphrase the title of Carl Becker's presidential address to the history profession in 1931), but every social scientist is his own behavioralist. Some are tool users, others are Truth-seekers; some want explanation, others prediction. In short, there is no agreement within the community of historians about their task. They lack a common way of seeing; hence they disagree on substantive issues of theory, method, and explanation. The traditional humanist paradigm is in jeopardy, but a behavioral consensus has not emerged.[36]

What are the gains and loses of social science history? On the assets side of the balance sheet, the social science influence has encouraged historians openly to state their assumptions and presupposi-tions, which formerly were often masked or supressed. Robert Fogel and Stanley Engerman, for example, began their study of the econom-ics of American slavery, *Time on the Cross,* with a summary list of the major conclusions and the cliometric methods and theoretical models on which they were based. Second, research design and methodology now receive far more attention than they did formerly, which encour-ages greater integrity among scholars in the use of evidence. Third, quantitative methods make it possible to study past societies "from the bottom up" by including the inarticulate masses who have usually been ignored in favor of the elites. Christian scholars who affirm the biblical principle of the worth of each person, great or small, can only applaud this inclusion in historical work of the little people of past societies.

These common folk are usually studied in groups or communities rather than as individuals, which gives rise to the charge that the social science approach dehumanizes history. But no man is an island. Indi-viduals exist in relationship—with family, ethnocultural groups, reli-gious communities, fellow workers, neighbors, and compatriots. To interpret the behavior of a particular individual, therefore, necessitates an understanding of the social groups within which that person lives and acts. Indeed, the study of social groups and their particular struc-tures is essential before one isolates for study individuals within those groups. To assess the voting record of Senator Harry S. Truman, for example, Gary Fink and James Hilty first analyzed the voting patterns of all Senators during Truman's career, and only then did they describe Truman's voting behavior in comparison to other major senatorial figures and the various constituencies and subgroups in the Senate.[37]

The debit side of the behavioral ledger is more difficult to assess because of the polemical nature of much of the critical literature. The main entries include, first, the charge that social science history leads to behavioral*ism,* to the Faustian pretense to total knowledge of human behavior, based solely on numbers. "In historical circles," says Kenneth Lockridge, this perception "leads to an image of Robert Fogel, in his laboratory amid swarms of scurrying assistants, crying through the steamy air, "numbers, numbers, give me numbers!"[38] This humorous "put-down" aside, behavioralists often do operate from a positivistic, rationalist base; they display an almost religious desire to redeem themselves through their own schemes of knowledge. H. Van Riessen has correctly observed that for many academics, "modern science is pre-eminently the means of self-redemption."[39] But this misplaced faith is not a condemnation of empirical methods per se. Theodore Rott-man, a Christian sociologist, has helped clarify this by distinguishing empiricism and positivism: to study past human behavior by rational methods of observation is to take God's world seriously. Although distorted by the Fall, people bear the Creator's image and, as social beings, engage in meaningful human interaction. One can study social relationships empirically without placing ultimate faith in rational methods and worshiping the results.[40]

Second, critics charge behavioralists with reductionism, breaking down complex problems into artificially contrived subparts for minute analysis, and thereby reducing human beings to behavior traits that are easiest to document by survey questionnaires.[41] "To put it bluntly," says Bernard Zylstra, "the social sciences are paying increasing attention to societal systems but less attention to human beings."[42] But reducing a complex issue into its component parts is quite appropriate and necessary, I believe, provided the problem is simplified intelligently and that literary sources are used in conjunction with behavioral data. Third, numerologists supposedly "bleach out the very soul of 'human existence' that is so desperately needed."[43] Numbers are by their very nature inhumane, it is charged. Lockridge has confronted this canard head-on: "I'm prepared to argue," he says, "that the way to a revival in history as a humanistic discipline lies precisely through the social scientific analysis of historical structures, shocking though this may seem. I would argue that it is through a knowledge of the demographic and social structures of the past that we gain the best and most accurate sense of what it means to be a man, or a woman."[44]

A fourth criticism, argued passionately if not cogently by Jacques Barzun, is that quanto-history is deterministic and mechanistic. Quantifiers, he avers, conceive of people and events as homogeneous units that can be described in facts and figures. These facts are then "shoveled . . . into the mouth of the minotaur" in the belief that "the garrulous machine could transmute their leaden data into golden truths."[45] While neophytes in the discipline might be guilty of fitting Barzun's caricature of simplistic thinking, trained practitioners are not. They realize the GIGO effect—garbage in, garbage out. They also have learned to expect the unexpected in research outcomes and to be satisfied if quantitative evidence illuminates only part, rather than the whole, of past reality.[46]

Another negative aspect of behavioral history is its tendency toward messianism: some behavioralists believe their mission to be the redemption of society. Scientific teleology envisions a society without conflict where everyone will enjoy personal peace and affluence. "Changing social science to change the world" was the remarkable title of Lee Benson's address to the 1977 conference of the Social Science History Association. Benson, the first president of the Association, lauded Karl Marx for demanding that "moral philosophers" ought to help create a better society. "I do accept his general prescription for what social scientists *ought* to do," Benson said. Their primary task is to develop "credible empirical theories about human behavior highly useful to human beings struggling to create a better world."[47] As one example of such beneficial uses, Benson doubtless had in mind his 1972 proposal for a billion-dollar, federally funded Violence Research Institute composed of social scientists who would "grapple seriously with the overall problem of human violence" and "develop good general theories about the causes, consequences, and control of violence for the 'benefit of Humane Life.'"[48]

Such a concerted effort by social scientists might possibly yield great scholarly dividends. But Benson's presuppositions, which he stated explicitly, should be noted: "As I conceive the concept, *intrasocietal* violence, it derives from the assumption that no such thing exists as an *innate* human instinct for aggression, hostility or violence. Aggressors are made, not born. . . . Granted that assumption, it follows that intrasocietal violence, from sporadic anomic violence to full-scale revolutions, *indicates that something is wrong with the society in which it occurs.* Violence threatens life, a condition contrary to human reason and human welfare. . . . It should be viewed and treated, therefore, as a symptom of societal rather than *individual* disorder."[49] Benson, in short, not only holds an optimistic view of the scientific method but believes that, since aggression is merely a symptom of society's malfunctioning, a favorable environment will lead to improved social morality. This analysis of the source of evil leaves no place for free will, for irrational actions, or for behavior conditioned by genetic or biological factors. It also rejects the Judaeo-Christian belief in the fallenness of humankind—in the innate human predisposition to evil. Social science ideologues such as Benson ultimately envision a society without conflict, one in which traditional aggressive behavior has become outmoded.[50]

Benson's activist agenda for the historical profession is not widely shared. Few historians aspire to such lofty heights. Most have little sympathy for dedicating the discipline to the quest for objective, durable "laws" of human behavior that may lead to a peaceful, cohesive society. Aydelotte correctly calls this "unrealistic."[51] Analytical and statistical methods borrowed from the social sciences aid in our understanding of past time, but they cannot solve the human dilemma now or in the future.

In summary we can make three assertions. First, statistics and computers are powerful tools that enable historians to tap new data sources and to explore new aspects of the past. Tools are not neutral instruments, of course, but if they acknowledge the tools' inherent biases and limitations, historians—including Christian historians—can properly use them.

Second, social scientific history is a companion, a complement, to traditional narrative history, rather than a substitute. I agree with Robert Fogel's statement that "neither mode of research by itself is adequate to deal with all the questions that concern historians."[52] Literary or ideational sources should be supplemented by serial or behavioral sources to clarify what is typical or aberrant, and to compare words with deeds, or opinions *about* behavior with *actual* behavior. It is wrong to draw too sharp a dichotomy between "science" and "history,"[53] between the positivist tradition of the Anglo-Saxon world and the idealist tradition of German historicism. Both, after all, have their origins in distorted versions of a Christian world view: the positivists emphasize natural laws and the idealists romanticize free will.[54] But Christian historians must recognize both fallenness and image-bearing, human freedom and divine control. There is both regularity and spontaneity in history. Human behavior is influenced by circumstances and also by individual actions freely undertaken. Our historical methods, therefore, must aid in generalizing and yet allow room for illuminating the unique. I affirm both commonality and individuality, without reconciling them. Empirical and traditional methods should coexist in creative tension.

Third, one can use behavioral methodology and social science theories without necessarily making a faith-commitment to behavioralism as a philosophy of life. The key is to use current models, theories, and techniques *critically* and *selectively*, recognizing the often humanistic assumptions and world views out of which they were developed, but also humbly acknowledging that non-Christian scholars have valid insights about human behavior and social relationships.[55] The alternatives to selective borrowing are less than satisfying. Antithetical thinking may lead to total rejection, and this would deny the truth that God permits unbelievers, by reason and observation, to gain valid knowledge about aspects of reality. The option of uncritical advocacy, as I indicated earlier, is clearly wrong. Another possible response is to develop a distinctively Christian social science. While I commend this option enthusiastically, I see little prospect of success in the near future. Christians in the behavioral sciences have only begun to think seriously about biblical norms in their disciplines.[56] This is the task before us.

8. Christianity, Christian Interpretation, and the Origins of the French Revolution

Dale Van Kley

Introduction

THE SUBJECT of this essay is not the experience of Christians and the Christian churches during the French Revolution, so ably and exhaustively studied by others.[1] Rather, it takes up the question of what possible relevance the Christian faith might have for the study of the French Revolution and for the formulation of properly historical judgments concerning it. The subject hence calls for an introductory word or two about both Christianity and the French Revolution.

If even the most impersonal varieties of history ultimately concern human beings and what they thought, said, and did in the past, then that part of the Christian faith most obviously relevant to history is its conception of human nature. Now the Christian conception of human nature is infinitely rich and profound, and one cannot aspire to do it justice within the scope of a paragraph or two. But the principal thing to note about it is precisely its complex and multifaceted quality. It does not present a "one-dimensional man." On the one hand, Christianity holds that people are created in God's own image, which implies that they are unique, in all creation, in their capacity both to know their creator and themselves as creatures, and to create, within limits, cultural worlds of their own. On the other hand, Christianity insists that humans, like the rest of creation, are finite, particular, and temporal, and that these characteristics are fundamentally good—because created—and essential to their nature. They are therefore neither God, nor beast, but human.

Again, Christianity on the one hand proclaims the highest calling for humans, that of God's representatives and viceroys in creation, implying in turn a life of obedience and love to their Creator. On the other hand, Christianity maintains that sin and evil have entered creation, and not by extraneous circumstance but by human responsibility. In revolt against their own finitude, they have aspired to be God; but by attempting to become much more than human, they have become considerably less than themselves. They now basely worship the products of their own perverted cleverness. Though they cannot but still be the crown of creation, they have become, in Pascal's words, the refuse of creation. They are dethroned kings, an enigma to themselves, alternately much worse and much better than they themselves could have anticipated.[2]

To continue with Pascal, one might therefore expect the Christian historian to abase humans whenever unduly exalted and to exalt them whenever unduly abased. If the intellectual historian, for example, makes people too much the master of their ideological destiny, their history too much the product of their self-conscious designs, then it is for the Christian institutional historian to point out the irony of human existence, how time and circumstance invariably distort the intentions of the most determined of founders, usually within their own lifetimes. And it is for the Christian economic historian to show people hungry and scared, the hapless victims of every absurd rumor that comes their way. But should the economic or social historian deny people's freedom, and make their actions uniquely the product of their material conditions and social situation, then it is for the Christian institutional or cultural historian to insist upon human freedom and responsibility, to point out that people had no small hand in the creation of the very material and social conditions that imprison and afflict them.

A second feature of Christianity that seems relevant is its historical character. Along with Judaism, it is an historical religion in the sense that its truth cannot be expressed except by reference to historical events. Christianity thus has the highest appreciation for the importance of the historical event. This is worth insisting on in the face of the historical profession's current denigration of narrative or event-history as merely "anecdotal," and its quasi-veneration of long-term social and economic trends, what Fernard Braudel has called the *longue durée*.[3] This is not, of course, to say that these are unimportant any more than, say, the long-term plan of God is unimportant in the history of salvation. But if the discrete event is unintelligible except in the light of the multisecular trend, the reverse seems equally true. And it is frequently the case that the long-term trend is importantly altered as a result of the unforeseen event, just as biblical evidence suggests that God might have changed his mind as a result of this or that occurrence.

As for the French Revolution, its historical importance would seem to speak for itself, especially if "history," as former President Nixon used to assure us, could record whatever it wished. Unhappily, it is not "history" but mere historians who do most of the recording, and in the case of the French Revolution they have been all too prolific. The literature concerning it is already Himalayan and seems to be growing more rapidly than ever. But not all parts of this mass have risen simultaneously or with equal speed. I therefore single out two facets for special attention, the first because of the overwhelming attention historians have recently given it, the second because of the benign (or malign) neglect with which they have recently ignored it. I speak of the *social* and *ideological* origins of the French Revolution.

The Tyranny of Sociology

Toward the beginning of the Third Republic, the French government instituted a professorial chair in the French Revolution at the Sorbonne. This has been a somewhat thankless business for the government, in the long run at least, because since the death of the original occupant, Alphonse Aulard, most of its titularies have been Marxists. These include the great Georges Lefebvre as well as the present occupant, Albert Soboul.

This fact hints at the extent to which Marxism, in France, has dominated the interpretation of the French Revolution—and the degree to which what happened in Russia in 1917 has colored the view of what happened in France in 1789. According to this view, the French Revolution of 1789 was a "bourgeois" or middle-class revolution which overthrew the theretofore dominant social class, the aristocracy, as well as its political arm, the Bourbon monarchy, and the remains of a socioeconomic system called "feudalism." The bourgeoisie's triumph had been preceded by centuries of inexorably growing economic strength based on commerce and industry, and by the eighteenth century its sheer economic power equaled and then outstripped the aristocracy's, based on landed wealth and feudal dues. Despite its steadily weakening economic base, the aristocracy retained political and social dominance until 1789, when the bourgeoisie seized these just rewards for economic power and cleared away the remaining "feudal" obstacles to the free development of capitalism. True, the bourgeoisie had recourse to the brawn of more popular social groups, notably the peasantry and the urban poor, to make good its victory, even though portions of these groups—harbingers of the proletariat—were not ultimately any more sympathetic to the bourgeoisie and capitalism than they were to the aristocracy and feudalism. All the same, the total Revolution is properly called a "bourgeois" revolution in terms of its consequences: the social and political triumph of the bourgeoisie and the untrammeled development of capitalism.[4]

The Marxist interpretation of the French Revolution got a valuable assist from American students of the Revolution during the 1950s and early 1960s. Without being Marxists themselves, these American scholars nonetheless agreed with the Marxists that the French Revolution was a bourgeois revolution. Their disagreement with the Marxist interpretation was mainly evaluative: whereas the Marxists ultimately deplored the bourgeois character of the Revolution—however required by the laws of the dialectic—the Americans welcomed the fact and wished it the happiest possible ever-afterdom.

The unique feature of the American contribution lay in its effort to explain why the French Revolution occurred precisely when it did, at the end of the eighteenth century. To this purpose, scholars such as Elinore Barber, Franklin Ford and—to a lesser extent—Robert Palmer developed and quite impressively documented the thesis of an "aristocratic reaction" in France at the end of the eighteenth century. What this thesis held, in short, was that throughout the eighteenth century, but especially toward its close, the French aristocracy, far from being prostrate and resignedly awaiting the guillotine, was actually rather rambunctious and indeed on the offensive on at least three fronts: politically against the monarchy, socially against the bourgeoisie, and economically against the peasantry.

Against the monarchy, the aristocracy pointed the resurgent political power of the French parlements, especially the Parlement of Paris, which in 1715 had regained its right to remonstrate against royal edicts and declarations prior to their registration. Firmly entrenched within these institutions, the aristocracy effectively blocked each and all of the monarchy's attempts to reform and modernize French institutions and society, and in particular to equalize the burden of taxation by whittling down the aristocracy's fiscal exemptions and privileges. It was the aristocracy through the parlements that in 1788 forced the monarchy to resurrect the long-defunct Estates-General, an event which, in the intentions of its perpetrators, was to undo the work of Richelieu, Mazarin, and Louis XIV and place the monarchy politically at the mercy of a revived aristocracy. The aristocracy was, moreover, all the more successful in its political offensive against the monarchy because at the same time—and on another and partly social front—it had stopped and even reversed the movement of the bourgeoisie into the royal bureaucracy and army and hence into the nobility itself. Gone was the heyday of the "vile bourgeoisie" which the crochety Duc de Saint-Simon had complained about during the reign of Louis XIV. Under the rule of his ineffective successor, the aristocracy came almost exclusively to staff the intendencies, the episcopacy, the officers' corps, and the magistracy, so that by the eve of the French Revolution the entire royal bureaucracy, broadly construed, was aristocratic. And since many of these offices and commissions, particularly those in the Parlement, conferred upon their occupants titles of nobility, their almost exclusive possession by those who were already noble had the effect of blocking existing avenues of upward social mobility for richer members of the bourgeoisie. That this was indeed the intended effect is attested by numbers of internal disciplinary regulations—by some of the parlements in the 1760s, by the officers' corps in 1781—requiring proof of four successive generations of nobility for admission by newcomers. The consequent accumulation of the bourgeoisie's social and psychological frustrations predictably exploded with revolutionary force in 1789 and thereafter.[5]

The economic dimension of the "aristocratic reaction," finally, took the form of turning the screws financially on the peasantry. Noble seigneurs tried to recoup their sagging fortunes and maintain their aristocratic extravagance by ransacking their archives for forgotten seigneurial dues and obligations and imposing these with rack-wrenching brutality upon a defenseless peasantry. The peasantry wreaked vengence in the summer of 1789 by destroying these archives and, often enough, the noble chateaux that housed them.[6]

Though the thesis of "aristocratic reaction" obviously recognized and attempted to account for the participation of groups like the nobility and the peasantry in the Revolution, it was above all the role of the ultimately triumphant bourgeoisie that it wished to underscore. Reflecting in large measure the sociological school of functionalism and in particular the sociology of Talcott Parsons, it thought of eighteenth-century French society as a sort of "system" whose stable functioning was jeopardized by weakening political controls: the ineffective monarchy of Louis XV and Louis XVI. The "aristocratic reaction" was then the proverbial monkey wrench that caused the "system" to develop fatal aristocratic "dysfunctions." The thesis was also typically American in that it reflected the American preoccupation with "social mobility" as the key to political stability—a notion anachronistically applied, perhaps, to a society in which most still viewed social mobility as the very nemesis of political stability.[7]

However persuasive and impressively documented, this entire Marxist or neo-Marxist edifice—along with its American flying buttress, the thesis of "aristocratic reaction"—has crumbled section by section in recent years, and there now seems very little of it left standing. It sustained its first serious blow when the late Professor Alfred Cobban of Cambridge University delivered his Wiles Lectures in 1962. Cobban pointed out, for example, that the French Revolution could hardly have destroyed "feudalism" in France, because "feudalism," properly defined, no longer existed in France to destroy. What the Revolution undoubtedly destroyed were elements of seigneurialism and manorialism—institutions both logically and historically separable from feudalism.[8] It was moreover the peasantry, not the bourgeoisie, that destroyed the remnants of seigneurialism during the "great fear" of July-August 1789, and in doing so, it also aimed at least a sidelong blow at agricultural capitalism, since capitalism, among the richer peasantry, was progressing precisely by means of the *seigneurie* (seigneurialism). For its part, the "revolutionary bourgeoisie"—that is, the delegates of the third estate then meeting at Versailles—did no more than legally ratify what the peasantry had already done, and reluctantly at that, since many of them were themselves *seigneurs* and collectors of seigneurial dues, this by no means being an exclusively noble affair. And if the Revolution somehow made straight the highway for the development of capitalism, the presumably capitalistic bourgeoisie seemed strangely reluctant to take to the road, since not only did commerce and industrial production fall off rather spectacularly during the revolutionary period, but capitalism remained a fairly lethargic business in France throughout much of the nineteenth century.[9] To the extent that capitalism flourished either before or after the Revolution, moreover, nobles had about as much to do with it as did the bourgeoisie.[10]

Perhaps the most important part of Cobban's work of destruction lies in its social analysis of the "revolutionary bourgeoisie"—that is, the delegates of the third estate who met in Versailles in May 1789, transformed the Estates-General into the National Assembly, proclaimed the rights of man and citizen, and so on.[11] Cobban noted that, far from the image of industrialists, financiers, and merchants which the term "bourgeoisie" naturally brings to mind, these delegates were in vast majority petty lawyers and owners of venal offices. They were already on the lower rungs of the ladder that eventually led to the status of nobility. On this point Cobban later received a valuable assist from George V. Taylor, who, in an analysis of the types of capitalism extant in eighteenth-century France, found that the bourgeoisie generally and the "revolutionary bourgeoisie" in particular tended to invest its wealth—however genuinely capitalistic in origin—in venal offices, land and *seigneuries,* and constituted *rentes* or annuities. All these forms of investment were typically aristocratic in that they involved little risk and were made ultimately for the purpose of acquiring social prestige and perpetuating the family and its noble style of life for as many generations as possible.[12]

But if no fundamental cleavage in forms of wealth existed between the "revolutionary bourgeoisie" and the aristocracy, then the conflict between them could hardly have been a class conflict if "class" be understood in anything like the Marxist sense of social groups occupying fundamentally different relationships to the means of production. Rather, their conflict appears to have been at most a glorified family quarrel, a mere status conflict.[13] This impression is reinforced by the very many studies in recent years that have emphasized the extent to which "privilege," as perhaps the chief constituent principle of the Old Regime, ran in one form or another from the top of society to the very bottom—or very nearly—and hence how misleading it is to think of the first and second estates as privileged and the third as not. On the one hand, portions of the nobility now seem to have been considerably less privileged than was thought heretofore—in the south, for example, they paid the main royal tax, or *taille*—and on the other hand, the bourgeoisie appears to have been comparatively more privileged, inasmuch as anyone rich enough could contrive to exempt himself from the *taille,* and usually did.[14] Viewed from an adequate social distance, the bourgeoisie and the nobility appear as two not very distinct segments of the French eighteenth-century elite, both ultimately living off revenues from the land. A genuine class distinction, if it existed at all, is rather to be found much lower in society: between those who worked with their hands and those who did not, or—perhaps not quite the same thing—between those who were economically independent and those whose economic condition was precarious and dependent.[15]

While Cobban, Taylor, and others were laying low the gothic heights of Marxist theory on the French Revolution, still others have gone destructively to work on the buttessing thesis of "aristocratic reaction," especially as it applies to the relationship between the bourgeoisie and nobility within the royal bureaucracy. Whereas that thesis had been based primarily on literary and legislative evidence, more recent studies of a statistical and social sort have begun producing a very different picture. A careful sampling of intendants from the reigns of Louis XIV, Louis XV, and Louis XVI has revealed, for example, that though nearly all of Louis XVI's intendants were nobles, all of Louis XV's and even Louis XIV's were too. More important, the percentage of nobles of very recent origin rose markedly from the close of the seventeenth century to the decade before the Revolution, a trend which represents an increase, not a decrease, in upward social mobility.[16] More recently still, an exhaustive numerical study focusing on the officers' corps of the army has similarly demonstrated that, though indeed only 5 to 6 percent of French army officers were commoners at the close of the Old Regime, things had never in fact been otherwise, and that the restrictive Ségur Law of 1781 requiring four quarterings of nobility was directed not against the bourgeoisie but against the growing number of rich candidates whose families had been more recently ennobled by means of other royal offices and dispensations. The same study took complete inventory of literally all those ennobled by these means during the fifteen years preceding the Revolution, and although the time span covered is not sufficiently long to demonstrate an actual increase in the rate of commoners entering the nobility in the course of the century, that is what it strongly suggests. At least, it shows that the governmental mechanisms of social ascension remained in good working order until the very end of the Old Regime. In this crucial domain, and at the level of "hard facts," there was apparently no "aristocratic reaction."[17]

The dust from all this destruction has not yet sufficiently settled to permit specialists in the history of the French Revolution to see too distinctly. As Thomas Kuhn would have it, we are "between paradigms"; the work of reconstruction has only tentatively begun.[18] Nonetheless, it seems possible, even at this early stage, to discern a few directions and perhaps suggest some others.

If, as now seems probable, no effective "aristocratic reaction" occurred in the domain of social mobility and at the level of "hard" social facts, it is worth recalling whatever led historians to posit such a hypothesis in the first place. Aside from the considerable force of theoretical predisposition, it was surely evidence of a legislative and literary sort: the rulings, for example, by some of the parlements noted earlier, requiring four generations of nobility for new members; protestations against noble snobbishness and seigneurial rapacity in the *cahiers de doléance* of 1789; and the antiaristocratic rhetoric of the later Revolution itself. Could it be, however, that this kind of evidence is valid and useful as far as it goes, that on psychological and political levels a species of "aristocratic reaction" indeed occurred? Might François Furet be correct in suggesting not only a rise in sheer noble snobbishness during the last half of the eighteenth century but, by ricochet, an exaggerated consciousness of difference between all social, professional, and corporate groups from the top of the social pyramid to its very base?[19] In this connection, one naturally thinks of the interminable squabbles over precedence in town religious processionals between this guild and that, these municipal officials and those royal officers; but also of the evermore resounding and often hollow jurisdictional clashes between the first and second orders of the clergy and between the parlements and practically everyone else: *bailliage* and *sénéchaussée* courts, intendants and provincial governors, the clergy, the provincial estates, and, of course, the royal council itself.

A more "open" society at the level of social and economic "reality," a more closed, differentiated, and punctilious society both mentally and politically—does such a paradoxical combination of features make any kind of social sense? Surely it does. For is it not possible that, in proportion as the things that had differentiated people heretofore progressively lost any real social and economic sense, people's initial reaction was anachronistically to accentuate these very differences? Threatened in their traditional identities by the march of social and economic facts, might not people have first reacted by noisily asserting their identities in the face of these facts—until that magic moment in 1789 when they thought they might exchange these identities for the simple but dignified title of "citizen" of the "nation"?[20] And if, in spite of its apparent newness, this line of thought seems strangely familiar, it should. For it was Alexis de Tocqueville who, in his *Old Regime and the French Revolution* more than a hundred years ago, insisted that eighteenth-century Frenchmen were never less able to get on with each other though more alike than ever before, and that the chasm between the two "classes" had never been wider, though to become a noble under Louis XVI had never been easier. An eighteenth-century "group individualism," he said, had preceded the more thoroughgoing atomic individualism of the nineteenth century.[21]

In attempting to explain the phenomenon, de Tocqueville also called attention to a since neglected political dimension of the origins of the French Revolution, namely, the state. De Tocqueville's state was, of course, not the mere creature of society—whether as political instrument of the dominant class or regulator of social functions—but the shaper of society. Possessed of a will all its own, driven forward by its insatiable hunger for money and power, it pulverized society and ultimately reshaped it in its own image. The provinces and their separate estates, the clergy, the guilds, the whole society of orders—all these institutions had medieval origins and arose quite independently of the state. But by the eighteenth century the monarchy, while virtually destroying some of these institutions, had fastened upon and in a sense reinforced others. In doing so, however, it distorted them and turned their original purposes to ones more in line with its own, these usually having to do with the royal fisc. It was the monarchy alone which, by the eighteenth century, had dispensed social prestige in the form of titles of nobility—which it did at a price. And if the monarchy reinforced the guilds and the few remaining provincial estates, it was in order indirectly to borrow money from the public.[22] The many conflicts between and within these institutions were thus not altogether what they seemed to be. Sapped of their original purposes by the monarchy, these orders and institutions fought in archaic garb over the quite modern issue of power and position within the state. Uncushioned by original flesh, the clashes between them were all the noisier for being clashes among skeletons. And though the state was in some sense the perpetrator of these conflicts, it was also their battleground—and victim, at least in its monarchical form. "Nothing," as de Tocqueville put it, "had been left that could obstruct the central government, but, by the same token, nothing could shore it up."[23]

This somewhat updated Tocquevillian vision is compelling to me personally, and it seems to represent which way the wind is blowing among specialists of the Revolution generally. Citations from de Tocqueville in the scholarly literature seem to be multiplying exponentially; Albert Soboul himself has been caught in the act of quoting from him.[24] It is, all the same, not my intention here to "Christianize" de Tocqueville or his *Old Regime*. The penultimate value that de Tocqueville placed on certain Romantic conceptions of political liberty and individuality, together with his willing subordination of religious loyalties to these, would prevent my doing so in any case.[25] What I would like to suggest, rather, is that in a general way Christian historians can legitimately take some comfort in the trend back toward a richer, more full-bodied conception of human experience.

In understandable but excessive reaction, no doubt, to a much older line of interpretation that emphasized the purely ideological origin of the French Revolution, the last several decades of theorizing about the Revolution's origins have been too exclusively and narrowly concerned with economics and sociology. The resulting eighteenth-century French universe has been stuffy and oppressive, inhabited by a species of creature uniquely preoccupied with getting rich and altering to his advantage his standing vis-à-vis his fellows. Now to deny that people are typically very concerned about these things would be foolish in the extreme. Instead, what is in question is whether "that is all there is"; and in partial but reassuring answer to this question, de Tocqueville and the recent trend in his direction reintroduce people who also build political institutions such as states, and are in turn molded by them. We thus can see that we inhabit a world of power and politics as well as of status and class; and a genuinely reciprocal relationship between political institutions, social relations, and economic conditions becomes conceivable.

The recent preoccupation with long-term social and economic trends has also tended to make the French Revolution all but unintelligible as *revolution*—that is, as radical departure or discontinuous event.[26] But need this be so? For combined, paradoxically, with a more traditional attention to the political event, these trends may illuminate it as never before. Take, for example, the Parlement of Paris's momentous decision on September 23, 1788, that the Estates-General should meet and vote by estate or order, as it had in days of yore, the last being 1614. Only against the backdrop of the long-term trend toward increasing social mobility can one appreciate its breathtakingly anachronistic quality, and hence how unintentionally it began to transform what had been at most diffuse bourgeois-noble tensions into the vitriolic anti-aristocratic rhetoric—the global condemnation of nobility as such, which characterizes so much of the revolutionary language. It was precisely the *conjonture*—to use a word dear to the *annales* school—of a long-term socioeconomic trend and a certain species of constitutional and political thinking in the form of an *event*—of all things—that began to radicalize, indeed revolutionize, the debate over the Estates-General. Precisely by flying impudently in the face of a social trend, by unceremoniously—or rather all too ceremoniously—throwing back all manner of legitimate social aspirants to nobility into the same archaic category with "vile" peasants, joiners, and cobblers, did this event crystallize theretofore amorphous social resentments and begin forging the slogans that carried the Revolution forward.[27]

The partial rehabilitation of de Tocqueville, the rediscovery of the political, and the "return of the event"—all these have been recently and provocatively combined in François Furet's *Penser la révolution française*. For it is exactly Furet's purpose to conceptualize or "think" the entire French Revolution as a dramatic event in which the "social" temporarily relinquished the leading role to the "political," and by "political" he means in part the competition among groups and persons for power within the vacuum created by the collapse of monarchical power in 1788. Groups competed for power, however, by claiming to articulate the will of the "nation," which in the new revolutionary parlance replaced the monarchy as absolute authority. Furet's concept of "political" thus includes or is at least adjacent to ideological, and so it reintroduces the question of the ideological origins of the French Revolution.[28]

The Ideological Origins of the French Revolution

Sociology, then, seems paradoxically to be liberating us from an exclusively social interpretation of the French Revolution; after a long eclipse, political history and the study of events are making a chastened and timid reappearance.[29] Is it too much to hope that ideas and religious loyalties will also resume their long relinquished place among the "causes" of the Revolution? Will the Revolution reacquire its ideological origins as well?

The ideological origins it was once thought to possess, of course, have mainly to do with the eighteenth-century intellectual movement known as the Enlightenment. From the time the French Revolution broke out, disgruntled opponents such as Edmund Burke and the Abbé Barruel pointed accusing fingers at a cluster of subversive ideas propagated by an equally subversive band of "effete impudent snobs and middle-aged malcontents." The ideas were those of deism and atheism, natural morality and *bienfaisance*, constitutional and representative government, national sovereignty and natural rights—in short, the Samson-like arms of nature and reason which together pulled down the twin pillars of throne and altar. The malevolent propagators were the likes of Voltaire, Montesquieu, Diderot, Rousseau, Helvetius—philosophers and encyclopedists generally. Though most of these culprits died before the Revolution itself, their doctrines survived them to make disciples who in turn both purposefully brought the Revolution about and guided its course thereafter.[30]

This, in embryo, was already the conservative "line" on the French

Revolution that, considerably nourished and enlarged upon by such
early nineteenth-century champions of monarchy and papacy as De
Maistre, Bonald, and Lamennais, persisted well into the twentieth
century and even today takes defiant refuge within the French Academy. In some of its manifestations, it attributed the outbreak of the
Revolution to a full-fledged plot hatched within the secrecy of Masonic
lodges; it also emphasized the foreign and specifically German prove-
nance of the ideas of the Enlightenment, stemming ultimately from the
Protestant Reformation and Luther's successful assertion of the principle of freedom of conscience. But whatever its individual vagaries, the
conservative interpretation of the Revolution darkly underscored the
role of the Enlightenment and regarded it as the chief if not the only
cause of the French Revolution—and of France's maladies ever since.[31]
Later in the century, interestingly enough, Groen van Prinsterer
adopted parts of this French Catholic and conservative litany and, with
Calvinistic responses, incorporated it into his lectures on the French
Revolution. It thus constitutes an element in the pristine ideology of
the Anti-Revolutionary party of the Netherlands.[32]

Beginning as early as Thomas Paine's reply to Edmund Burke in
1791, the liberal response to the conservative interpretation of the
French Revolution has consistently been to downplay the importance
of the Enlightenment in bringing about the Revolution and to emphasize, rather, the role of the concrete abuses and injustices of the Old
Regime and the specific circumstances that brought it down, such as
the bad harvest of 1788 and the financial crisis of the monarchy.[33]
Though the French liberal tradition has proudly identified with the
ideals of the French Revolution to the extent that these included
national sovereignty and constitutional government, its historians—
Thiers, Mignet, Michelet, Aulard—have paradoxically taken pains to
demonstrate that the Revolution was not the result of the conscious
intentions, much less a plot, on the part of those imbued with these
ideals, and that the ideals themselves were not as impractical, utopian—
indeed as idealistic—as Burke and others said they were.[34] Yet the
liberal interpretation of the French Revolution never totally denied a
causal role to the ideas of the Enlightenment. Throughout the nineteenth century and until the recent rise of the sociological school into
which it has been largely absorbed, the liberal tradition never really
questioned "this conclusion"—in the words of Daniel Mornet—"that it
is, in part, the ideas [of the Enlightenment] which brought about the
French Revolution."[35]

The publication, in 1933, of Daniel Mornet's *Les origines intellectuelles de la révolution française* marked in many ways the culmination of
the liberal treatment of this subject. At the same time it surpassed the
liberal tradition and still merits the attention and respect of professional

historians because of its impressive display of erudition and methodological scrupulousness. A product of ten years of research, the work
attempts to measure the spread of Enlightenment ideas geographically,
chronologically, and socially by paying careful attention not just to Paris
and intellectual figures of the first order but to provincial newspapers,
colleges, academies, and private libraries as well as to intellectuals of
the second, third, and still lower orders. In recent years the book has
sustained some criticism of a somewhat picayune, methodological sort;
but its chief defect is surely conceptual in nature. Mornet never seriously asked the question, What were the intellectual origins of the
French Revolution? Rather, he assumed from the very outset that they
were to be found exclusively within the Enlightenment, which he
narrowly defined in terms of the ideas of its principal representatives,
and then proceeded to look for their "influences."

Not surprisingly, he found them everywhere, especially since his
originally discrete and sharply delineated ideas tended to dissolve and
diffuse, once they were launched upon the stream of events, into a
ubiquitous "intelligence" manifesting itself as any sort of critical attitude
toward the regime. What emerged is an image of a purely receptive
tabula rasa called eighteenth-century France upon which the Enlightenment impressed whatever simple ideas it chose.

Mornet is still respectfully read by historians today mainly because
of his show of methodological rigor, because he took the bother to
count and measure instead of trusting mere impressions. And he was
one of the first to apply the methodology of public opinion polls to
the study of intellectual history. He is hence regarded as a precursor of
the kind of intellectual history very much in vogue these days, called
the social history of ideas.[36]

To call the social history of ideas a kind of intellectual history is
perhaps to stretch the meaning of terms, because it is only tangentially
interested in the content of books or ideas generally. Rather, the aim
of this enterprise is to situate the expression of ideas as precisely as
possible within its social setting, and to do this it insists on a good deal
of counting and plotting.[37] Take, for example, that most famous of
eighteenth-century philosophical productions, the *Encyclopédie* of Diderot and d'Alembert. In contrast to the traditional intellectual historian's preoccupation with the *Encyclopédie's* subversive message, the social
historian of ideas is more interested in the collective socioeconomic
and professional profile of the work's contributors or subscribers. Whatever the results of his inquiry, the intended effect is to anchor the
Englightenment enterprise on hard social and geographical bedrock.

There is no gainsaying the results of the social history of ideas.
For eighteenth-century France in particular, its achievements have been
most impressive, especially by way of introducing a new rigor into our

conceptions of the social import, content, underpinnings, and circula-
tion—as well as geographical distribution—of enlightened thought.
And though the genre is not completely innocent of a hidden agenda
in the form of the wholly gratuitous assumption that the socioeconomic
dimension of human experience is primary and foundational, the
intellectual one secondary and derivative, the main results of its en-
deavors have ironically served to scuttle such unseaworthy reductionism, especially in the form of the Marxists' regarding the Enlightenment
as the ideological expression of a rising industrial and commercial
bourgeoisie. Manufacturers and large-scale merchants are mainly "absent" from Jacques Proust's reconstituted list of contributors to the
Encyclopédie, who consisted massively of "*bourgeoisie d'ancien régime,*" that
is, *a bourgeoisie* "living essentially on revenues from land, offices, and
pensions," "profoundly integrated into the feudal system" and therefore
also "privileged"—this from a Marxist, trying as he may to put a good
face on the matter![38] Nobles of the robe and sword, Catholic clergymen,
and of course *bourgeoisie d'ancien régime* made up the crushing majority
of the *Encyclopédie's* subscribers in the city of Besançon and the surrounding province of Franche-Compté examined by Robert Darnton;
in general, the *Encyclopédie* sold much better in judicial, administrative,
and ecclesiastical cities such as Besançon or Toulouse than it did in
manufacturing or port cities such as Lille or Nantes. Businessmen
themselves, the booksellers knew that businessmen were among the
Encyclopédie's worst customers.[39] A similar pattern emerges from the geographical distribution and socioprofessional composition of the provincial academies so exhaustively analyzed by Daniel Roche.[40] In
largely ignoring, however, the content and message of the Enlightenment, these inquiries have all but abandoned—and have done little
even incidentally to clarify—the question that still interested Mornet,
namely, the role of ideas in bringing about the French Revolution.

I say "all but abandoned" because exceptions exist. One is Robert
Darnton, a practitioner of the social history of ideas, whose refreshingly
bold and imaginative speculations have attracted a great deal of notice
of late. Darnton has focused his attention on the second generation of
philosophers, more particularly on the second-, third-, and even tenth-
rate intellectuals such as Brissot and Marat, who tried to make it as
writers in the decades immediately preceding the Revolution and who
later surfaced spectacularly as leaders in the Revolution itself. Attracted
in increasing numbers from the provinces to Paris by the Voltairean
myth of a new "republic of letters" in which talent and industry alone
procured success, these men discovered to their chagrin that privilege
and the right social connections were as indispensable in this world as
in any other, and that a man could not live on the "bread" of his
writings alone. Rebuffed and embittered, they congregated and multi-

plied in "Grub Street," where they prostituted their talents as part-time police spies and as writers and peddlers of pornography. They learned to hate in their very guts the society that had thus corrupted them. Identifying much more with the outcast Rousseau than with the patrician Voltaire, they ran the Genevan's thought through the hard wringers of their own literary failure and degradation until it emerged as a *Rousseau du ruisseau,* an undiscriminating hatred of everything remotely distinguished or exalted. Whereas the "high" Enlightenment of Voltaire and Montesquieu might have gently and indirectly undermined respect for established order, enlightened thought as refracted through their bitter grubstreet experience provided at least some of the visceral and destructive hatred that more directly tore that order down.[41]

Or is this to put words in Darnton's mouth? For it is far from clear precisely what relationship he wishes to posit between his overpopulated Grub Street and the Revolution. Certainly Darnton's work throws a brilliant light on the heretofore obscure prerevolutionary experience of a Marat, Brissot, or Carra—in short, a certain type of disgruntled, low-grade intellectual—who figured so prominently in the Revolution itself; and he further suggests the role that this sort of personality might play in revolutions generally. But Darnton clearly wants to say more than that revolutions are the sorts of occurrences that throw to the surface disgruntled and unemployed intellectuals; he also wants to say that unemployed and disgruntled intellectuals are the sorts of people who help bring about revolutions. Yet in response to the question of how they did so in this instance, he unfortunately becomes unclear and talks vaguely of their having "spread disaffection deeper and more widely" and having provided the authentic voice of Jacobinism.[42] Aside from noting his lack of a precise documentation for these assertions, one is tempted to paraphrase a remark Albert Soboul made in a different context altogether, to the effect that revolutions are not typically made by prostitutes, police spies, pornographers, and the like.[43]

Is it possible that Mornet looks too "high," and Darnton too "low," for the ideological origins of the Revolution? Certain it is, in any event, that what principally fixed the attention of Frenchmen during much of the eighteenth century was not the comings and goings of Voltaire, the imprisonment of Diderot, or the publication of the *Encyclopédie,* but rather the mixed political, ecclesiastical, and religious controversies related to Jansenism, the papal bull *Unigenitus,* the Jesuit Order, and the Parlement of Paris's right to nullify and control the monarchy's legislative acts.[44]

The origins of these controversies lie most specifically in the seventeenth century. The movement of theological and ecclesiastical reform called Jansenism, which first attracted notice in France in the 1640s and 1650s, was originally a part of the larger French Catholic

Counter Reformation and barely distinguishable from it. But its austere morality and uncompromising emphasis on the Augustinian doctrines of gratuitous predestination and efficacious grace made it vulnerable to the charge of crypto-Calvinism and brought it inevitably into conflict with the institutional spearhead of the Counter Reformation, the Jesuit Order, which was powerful both in Rome and in the French court. Partly owing to Jesuitical influence, the papacy condemned Jansenist doctrines in a series of encyclicals and bulls, and a nervous French monarchy, worried that Jansenist independence and accent on the individual conscience undermined the laws of hierarchy and subordination, lent the wholehearted support of the "secular sword."

Persecuted by Rome, the monarchy, and the larger part of the French episcopacy, Jansenism sought and obtained a certain protection from the Parlement of Paris, which was motivated for its part by the concern that the papacy was suing Jansenism as a pretext for threatening the traditional independence of the French or Gallican Church. But as interpreted by the Parlement's magistrates and legists, this Gallican tradition meant not only the Gallican Church's right to abide by its own usages and to judge doctrine concurrently with Rome, but also the state's right to curtail the independence of the church and enforce conformity to its own canons—even against the episcopacy, if the Parlement deemed this necessary. At about the same time, moreover, the Parlement found itself locked in mortal combat with the monarchy during the civil war known as the Fronde. Among the issues at stake was the constitutional one of whether the Parlement, as presumed successor to the defunct Estates-General, the medieval court of peers, and even Charlemagne's yearly meetings with his barons, had the right to negate, modify or freely consent to the royal edicts and declarations sent to it for regulation.[45]

It was hence fortuitous historical circumstance, a common opposition to papacy, episcopacy, and monarchy, that first brought the heterogeneous elements of Jansenism, Gallicanism, and parlementary constitutional pretensions together.[46] It was the bull *Unigenitus*, the last and most important of the papal bulls condemning Jansenism, that welded them into a coherent oppositional point of view. Solicited by the aging and increasingly bigoted Louis XIV, and promulgated by Clement XI in 1713, this bull stupidly offended both Augustinian and Gallican susceptibilities, and elicited not only the predictable hostility of the Parlement of Paris but of a sizable proportion of the episcopacy as well. But the monarchy had engaged its authority in behalf of the bull, and it persisted in its attempt to enforce it as a law of church and state. It gradually weeded out opponents of the bull from the episcopacy, expelled them wholesale from the Sorbonne, and exerted unremitting pressure on the Parlement of Paris to register it without reservations. But these actions served only to exacerbate the hostility and swell the ranks of the opponents, who responded with a deluge of clandestinely printed pamphlets. This and related controversies so dominated the French scene, at least until the 1770s, that the whole eighteenth century in France might just as well be called the century of *Unigenitus* as the century of lights.[47]

The Jansenist-Gallican and parlementary mentality of opposition which the monarchy thereby created somehow exceeded the sum of its component parts. In the name of doctrinal Augustinianism, it denounced the heretical Pelagianism and perverse morality of the Jesuit Order and called upon all good Catholics to uproot them. In the name of episcopal Gallicanism, it denounced the "foreign" influences of the Jesuit order and the Jesuit-dominated papacy, and called upon the "nation" and "all good Frenchmen" to eradicate them. In the name of parlementary Gallicanism, it denounced the "spirit of domination" and "system of independence" of the Gallican bishops and their vicars, and called upon the monarchy to subjugate them. And in the name of parlementary constitutionalism, it denounced the "despotism" and arbitrariness of this same monarchy—of at least its ministers—and called upon all good "patriots" to oppose them. Nor did accomplishments lag behind rhetoric. By means of its institutional stronghold within the Parlement of Paris, this Gallican-Jansenist opposition succeeded in wresting control of the sacraments from the episcopacy in the 1750s and suppressing the Jesuit Order in the 1760s, and it raised such a hue and cry against the "despotism" of Chancellor Maupeou's suppression of the parlements in 1771 that Louis XVI felt obliged to restore them upon his accession in 1775.[48]

On the other side of the conflict, the "devout party" within the court, the Jesuit Order and a militant group within the episcopacy, were far from inactive. Through most of the eighteenth century the monarchy obligingly responded to the militant bishops' pleas to protect "religion"—and to reinforce their control over the second order of the clergy—with a shower of blessings in the form of *lettres de cachet* against Jansenist priests and others; and it piously retreated after Comptroller-General Machault's attempt to end the Gallican Church's fiscal immunities elicited an episcopal litany of woe in 1750. It was not until a militant episcopal group led by the Archbishop of Paris launched an ultimately unsuccessful attempt to extirpate Jansenism from the ranks of the lower clergy by systematically refusing the sacraments of the Eucharist and extreme unction to opponents of the bull *Unigenitus* that relations between the monarchy and the bishops showed signs of real strain. The strain developed into something close to open rupture when Louis XV failed to save the Jesuits from the Jansenist-Gallican assault on them during the 1760s.[49]

It was then—during the 1750s and 1760s—that the bishops raised the cry of alarm at the spread of irreligion in France and began to talk darkly of the woeful consequences of a disunited throne and altar in the face of it. The cause of true religion, to hear them tell it, had not been in more dire straits since the worst persecutions under the Roman Empire; fire, dungeon, and sword were just around the corner, and they pronounced themselves fully prepared for these trials. Indeed, they seemed to develop from this moment a genuine persecution complex, and to go into training, as it were, for the all too real persecutions some of them were later to sustain during the Revolution itself.[50] In embarrassed reaction, moreover, to the unremitting barrage of shrill Gallican rhetoric directed against them, a number of bishops began explicitly to distance themselves from the Gallican tradition of independence from Rome which their seventeenth-century predecessors had helped define, and to fly into the waiting arms of the papacy. They became ultramontanists, some of them more papist than the pope. And to warn the monarchy against cooperation with the "heretical" parlements, episcopal pamphleteers began to harp on the subversive nature of parlementary constitutionalism, to refer ominously to Cromwell and Charles I, and to advance theories of monarchy fully as despotic as their enemies feared. By mid-century, a part of episcopal France was already more royalist than the king.[51]

Recall now the nineteenth century's conflicting "liberal" and "conservative" interpretations of the French Revolution. It goes without saying that these conflicting interpretations of the immediate past were laden with contemporary political significance, that they reflected the political and religious divisions that nineteenth-century French society had inherited from the Revolution. "Liberal" France, which accepted the Revolution's assertion of national sovereignty and constitutional government, squared off against "conservative" France, which rejected both in the name of throne and altar, divine-right monarchy, and ultramontanist Catholicism.[52] But are not these modern divisions already quite discernible in the mixed religious, ecclesiastical, and political controversies of the mid-eighteenth century? Is not "liberal" France already visible, if only in embryonic form, in the appeal to the "nation" and to "patriots," and beneath the archaic constitutionalism, of the Jansenist-Gallican-parlementary alliance? And does not the Archbishop of Paris or the Bishop of Orléans already anathematize in the very accents of a Lamennais or De Maistre? The Marquis d'Argenson could not have been more perspicacious when he observed, of these mid-eighteenth-century controversies, that they no longer so much pitted Jansenists against Molinists as nationals against sacerdotals.[53]

If there is anything to this, then the mixed religious, ecclesiastical, and political controversies of the mid-eighteenth century contain the ideological origins not only of the Revolution but of the Counter Revolution as well. And the Revolution is then in part the product of the ideological divisions of modern France, as well as a progenitor of them in its turn. This is, of course, not to deny that both of these fundamental political directions were importantly modified in the course of the later eighteenth century by way of contact with concrete events and the wider context of enlightened thought. Conspicuously missing, for example, in mid-eighteenth-century Gallican and parlementary constitutionalism, are the egalitarianism and notions of individual representation that were later acquired from the example of the American Revolution and the progressive breakdown in France itself of the society of corporations and orders. But it is indeed to assert that at mid-eighteenth century these divisions existed quite apart from anything very specifically "enlightened." The divisions existed within Catholicism; they did not by themselves divide Catholic from unbeliever. To the extent that they were employed, typically "enlightened" sorts of arguments such as appeals to reason, experience, or some primitive contract were employed on either side of the argument, not just one.[54] In other words, the Enlightenment did not by itself create the fundamental political and ideological divisions of modern French society, but rather provided the conceptual apparatus and vocabulary in which these were progressively expressed.[55]

But what, then, of the unbelievers? What of the anti-Catholic—indeed anti-Christian—Enlightenment of Voltaire, Montesquieu, and Rousseau, the atheistic one of Diderot and d'Holbach? If, as I have had the temerity to argue, this phenomenon does not altogether deserve the lion's share it has traditionally received among the ideological origins of the Revolution, it is worth asking, once again, whatever led historians to accord it as much attention in the first place. Surely, in part, it was the rhetoric of eighteenth-century defenders of the faith—in the 1750s the bishops were already taxing their Gallican and Jansenist forces with "unbelief"—but above all the Revolution's abolition of the Christian calendar, the transformation of churches into temples of reason, the defrocking of priests and lay "debaptisations"—in a word, the spectacular "de-Christianization" campaign of the revolutionary year II (1793–4). This shocking phenomenon convinced most contemporaries as well as historians ever since that the ideological origins of the Revolution as a whole could only be traced to the impious Voltaire and the deistic Rousseau, whose remains the Revolution reverently transferred to the Pantheon (formerly the Church of St. Geneviève).

But just as in the case of the Revolution's antiaristocratic rhetoric, it is inadmissible to read back into the eighteenth century what is in large measure a product of the revolutionary event itself, and to morsel up, so to speak, one's treatment of the eighteenth century so as to be the more conveniently digested by the year 1789 or 1793. The story of the Civil Constitution of the Clergy, and how the Gallican Church and the Revolution came to blows in consequence, is well known and need not be retold here, except to say that it is a story of tragic and largely unforeseeable blunders and miscalculations, as a result of which the most extreme reactions on either side came to define normal relations between them.[56] In the process, the revolutionary mentality came to identify the priest along with the aristocrat as a symbol of Counter Revolution, and reacted, in part, with the most virulent from of anticlericalism available.[57] Consequently, even the many patriotic priests who had accepted the Revolution were driven into the arms of papacy and Counter Revolution.[58] It was hence again the contingent event of the Revolution, and this alone, that refracted the antecedent division between papacy and royalty on the one side, nation and constitution on the other, into one of Catholic and unbeliever as well. The resulting revolutionary thorns and thistles have been noxious indeed. They explain why the few nineteenth-century attempts at "liberal" Catholicism were so quickly choked out, and why the combination of Catholic piety and loyalty to the republic has been so hard to come by in France, even to the present day.

If, finally, this line of interpretation contributes anything to a Christian understanding of the French Revolution, it consists in its sufficiently enlarging the dimensions of human experience to take people's ideas seriously, in insisting that people build political institutions and compete for power not merely for their own sakes, but as a means to implement these ideas. In insisting as well that at least in this instance these ideas had religious and ecclesiastical origins, this interpretation beckons "ecclesiastical" or "church" history out of its self-imposed ghetto and invites it to claim its place in the very thick of things, where it surely belongs.

However unrelated the two parts of this essay might appear, they touch at several points.

For one thing, the first part's conflicts among the Old Regime's corps and corporations as well as within its social hierarchy contributed importantly to the ideological divisions discussed in the second. For the Old Regime's two major corporations, the parlement and the clergy, were thoroughly intertwined in the mixed religious, ecclesiastical, and political controversies that produced the modern division between nation and constitution on the one side, throne and altar on the other. And though before the Revolution it had not divided Catholic from unbeliever, the divisions so interacted in turn with the fallout from the exploding social hierarchy during the Revolution itself that they associated Catholicism as a whole with aristocracy, and unbelief with the cause of equality. The result was two opposing configurations of loyalties that grouped nation, constitution, equality, and unbelief against papacy, monarchy, hierarchy, and Catholic piety.

The contingent event, moreover, played a crucial role in both sections: that is, in the processes of both social disintegration and ideological formation as well as in the complex interactions between these two. Too simple though this whole scheme undoubtedly is, it is hence more contingent and more irreducibly complex than those regnant heretofore, and this, I submit, is the direction in which we should move.

Notes

Chapter 2 C. T. McIntire

1. Herbert Butterfield, *The Origins of History* (New York: Basic Books, 1981).

2. See Herman Strasser and Susan C. Randall, *An Introduction to Theories of Social Change* (London and Boston: Routledge and Kegan Paul, 1981); and Alfred Schmidt, *History and Structure: an Essay on Hegelian-Marxist and Structuralist Theories of History* (Cambridge: MIT Press, 1981).

3. See Michael Kammen, ed., *The Past Before Us: Contemporary Historical Writing in the United States* (Ithaca: Cornell University Press, for the American Historical Association, 1980). Ernst Breisach, *Historiography: Ancient, Medieval, and Modern* (Chicago: University of Chicago Press, 1983), provides an insightful historical explanation of this proliferation of types of histories.

4. See, e.g., Hendrik Hart, *Understanding Our World: Toward an Integral Ontology* (Washington: University Press of America, 1984); Nicholas Wolterstorff, *On Universals* (Chicago: University of Chicago Press, 1970).

5. Colossians 1:1–21. The Gospel of Matthew emphasizes the theme of the coming of the rule of God. St. Augustine proposed a way to connect biblical history with postbiblical history around the theme of the City of God.

6. I shall not explore anything of the history of our human understanding of time, but I can recommend two excellent books as an introduction to the theme: J. T. Fraser, *The Voices of Time* (2nd ed.; Amherst: University of Massachusetts Press, 1981); and Charles M. Sherover, *The Human Experience of Time: The Development of Its Philosophical Meaning* (New York: New York University Press, 1975).

7. Marc Bloch, *The Historian's Craft* (New York: Vintage, 1953), chapter 1, "History, Men, and Time"; Eric Hobsbawn, "From Social History to the History of Society," and François Furret, "Quantification History," both in *Historical Studies Today,* edited by Felix Gilbert and Stephen R. Graubard (New York: W. W. Norton, 1972), pp. 10–11, 54–55.

8. Robert F. Berkhofer, Jr., *A Behavioral Approach to Historical Analysis* (New York: The Free Press, 1969), p. 211. Berkhofer devotes two thick chapters to the theme.

9. John Mbiti, *African Religions and Philosophy* (London: Heinemann, 1969), pp. 19–21.

10. Romans 6:8–10; cf. Hebrews 10. Augustine, *City of God*, XII, 15. See *Herbert Butterfield: Writings on Christianity and History,* edited by C. T. McIntire (New York: Oxford University Press, 1979), pp. 124–130.

11. See *Bhagavad Gita,* VI, 40–45; IV, 5–9.

12. Genesis 2:8–3:24; and Revelation 21. See Mircea Eliade, *Cosmos and History: The Myth of the Eternal Return* (New York: Harper and Row, [1954], 1959). In my opinion, Eliade is mistaken in viewing the Christian understanding of a new heaven and new earth as an example of eternal return to a Golden Age of Paradise.

13. See Erik Erikson's famous chapter, "The Eight Ages of Man," in

Childhood and Society (2nd ed.; New York: Norton, 1963); see also Theda Skocpol, *States and Social Revolutions: A Comparative Analysis of France, Russia, and China* (Cambridge: Cambridge University Press, 1979).

14. For example, Frank E. Manuel, *Shapes of Philosophical History* (Stanford: Stanford University Press, 1965); and David Bebbington, *Patterns in History: A Christian View* (Downers Grove, Illinois: InterVarsity Press, 1979).

15. See C. T. McIntire, *England against the Papacy, 1858–1861* (Cambridge: Cambridge University Press, 1983).

16. The similarity of kinds of processes is the source of cyclical theories of civilization, like Arnold Toynbee's *A Study of History,* 12 vols. (Oxford: Oxford University Press, 1934–1961), but also of all social, economic, and political prediction.

17. See Herbert Butterfield, *Origins of History.*

18. Wolfhart Pannenberg, *Theology and the Kingdom of God* (Philadelphia: Westminster, 1969), pp. 53–55.

19. Herman Dooyeweerd makes this point very well in *A New Critique of Theoretical Thought* (Philadelphia: Presbyterian and Reformed, 1953–1958), I, 22–34. I note my general debt to Dooyeweerd's modal theory, although I would revise it substantially.

20. See Kevin Lynch, *What Time is This Place?* (Cambridge: MIT Press, 1972); and especially J. T. Fraser, *Voices of Time.* Both books, Lynch for Boston and Fraser for the academic disciplines, show how diverse the manifestations of time can be.

21. See, for example, Emmanuel Le Roy Ladurie and Paul Dumont, "Quantitative and Cartographical Exploitation of French Military Archives, 1819–1826," *Historical Studies Today,* pp. 62–106.

22. In English, the two senses of our usage of the word "being" indicate the structural and the historical dimensions of the same phenomenon at the same moment, as in: I am a human being (structural); and I am being human (historical).

23. See Robert A. Nisbet, *Social Change and History: Aspects of the Western Theory of Development* (New York: Oxford University Press, 1969).

24. See Genesis 1:26–30; 2:15–25. As I understand our cultural mandate, we have no call to exploit wantonly the nonhuman creatures, but to work with them in ways that respect their own integrity and their response to God. The accent in the cultural mandate is not on aggressiveness but on creativity and care.

25. See Berkhofer, *A Behavioral Approach,* chapters 4–7; see also Berkhofer, "Clio and the Culture Concept: Some Impressions of a Changing Relationship in American Historiography," *Social Science Quarterly,* 53 (1972), 297–320; see also Clifford Geertz, *The Interpretation of Cultures: Selected Essays* (New York: Basic Books, 1973).

26. W. H. Walsh uses the term "colligation" to refer to the discovery and articulation of relationships. My suggestion may be seen as involving four kinds of colligation. Walsh, *Philosophy of History: An Introduction* (rev. ed.; New York: Harper and Row, 1967).

Chapter 3   Martin E. Marty

1. E. P. Thompson, *The Making of the English Working Class* (New York: Pantheon, 1964), p. 371 and *passim.*

2. Frederick A. Olafson, *The Dialectic of Action: A Philosophical Interpretation of History and the Humanities* (Chicago: University of Chicago Press, 1979); on "agent's description," see chapter 4, "Historical Narrative," pp. 133–188.

3. Erik Erikson, *Young Man Luther* (New York: Norton, 1968).

4. Jacob Burckhardt, *Force and Freedom: An Interpretation of History* (New York: Meridian, 1955), p. 72.

5. Nicholas Berdyaev, *The Meaning of History* (Cleveland: Meridian, 1962); M. C. D'Arcy, S.J., *The Meaning and Matter of History: A Christian View* (Cleveland: Meridian, 1959); Karl Löwith, *Meaning in History* (Chicago: University of Chicago Press, 1957); Henri-Irèneé Marrou, *The Meaning of History* (Baltimore: Helicon, 1966).

6. Christopher Dawson, *The Dynamics of World History* (New York: Mentor, 1956).

7. William H. Dray, *Philosophy of History* (Englewood Cliffs, N.J.: Prentice-Hall, 1964). Chapter 7, "An Empirical Approach," pp. 82–97, treats Toynbee as an empirical understanding; see Arnold J. Toynbee, *A Study of History* (New York: Oxford University Press, ten volumes, 1934–1954).

8. The "Omega Point" theme courses through and unifies the whole Teilhardian corpus.

9. Arthur J. Danto, *Analytical Philosophy of History* (Cambridge: Cambridge University Press, 1965), pp. 1, 7, 9, 11, 13f.

10. See, for example, William G. McLoughlin, Jr., *Modern Revivalism: Charles Grandison Finney to Billy Graham* (New York: Ronald Press, 1959). McLoughlin has since written biographies of Billy Sunday, Billy Graham, and Henry Ward Beecher along with more synthetic works on revivalism.

11. Danto, pp. 15, 19.

12. On "traces," see G. J. Renier, *History: Its Purpose and Method* (Boston: Beacon, 1950), pp. 96–105.

13. A. J. Ayer, *Language, Truth and Logic* (London: Victor Gollancz, 1936), p. 115.

14. Frederick Ferré, *Language, Logic and God* (New York: Harper and Brothers, 1961), pp. 61, 63.

15. See J. H. Plumb, "This Historian's Dilemma" in J. H. Plumb, ed., *Crisis in the Humanities* (Baltimore: Penguin, 1964), pp. 24–44 for a plaintive appeal that "progress" be reintroduced as a doctrine to thread historical writing together.

16. See Walter von Loewenich, *Luther's Theology of the Cross* (Minneapolis: Augsburg, 1976) and John Headley, *Luther's View of Church History* (New Haven: Yale, 1963).

17. See Headley, p. 46.

18. Renier, p. 14.

Chapter 4   George Marsden

1. See, for example, C. T. McIntire, ed., *God, History and Historians* (New York, 1977), and George Marsden and Frank Roberts, eds., *A Christian View of History?* (Grand Rapids, 1975). See especially the bibliographical essay by M. Howard Rienstra, pp. 181–196.

Dirk Jellema correctly points out that the dilemma I pose has often been addressed by Christian commentators as for example in terms of "neutral" tools of history that may serve either of two kingdoms or in terms of "common grace" in the Calvinist tradition. His essay "'Why Study History?' Mused Clio," *A Christian View of History?* pp. 17–29, discusses such approaches.

2. See especially Becker, *Everyman His Own Historian: Essays on History and Politics* (Chicago, 1935); *The Heavenly City of the Eighteenth-Century Philosophers* (New Haven, 1932).

3. Thomas S. Kuhn, *The Structure of Scientific Revolution* (2nd ed.; Chicago, 1970 [1962]).

4. "A Christian Perspective for the Teaching of History," *A Christian View of History?* pp. 35–36.

5. Reid says: "The faculties which nature has given us, are the only engines we can use to find out the truth. We cannot indeed prove that those faculties are not fallacious, unless God should give us new faculties to sit in judgment upon the old. But we are born under a necessity of trusting them.

"Every man in his senses believes his eyes, his ears, and his other senses. He believes his consciousness, with respect to his own thoughts and purposes, his memory, with regard to what is past, his understanding, with regard to what is elegant and beautiful." *Essays on the Active Powers of the Human Mind*, II, ii, 6; Baruch A. Brody, ed. (Cambridge, Mass., 1969 [1788]), p. 237.

6. Whether what we learn qualifies as certain "knowledge" is a question tortured in philosophical debates. I think Reid considered these mechanisms to yield knowledge. He often makes the point that such "probable demonstrations" can be virtually as certain as the deductions of logic. However, if we describe these mechanisms involved as "truth-conducive," we avoid certain problems of being justifiably sure about certain beliefs that turn out to have been built on misconceptions. Generally, I do not use "knowledge" in the philosophers' strict sense that involves being both certain and right.

7. Becker says: "Let us then admit that there are two histories: the actual series of events that once occurred; and the ideal series that we affirm and hold in memory. The first is absolute and unchanged—it was what it was whatever we do or say about it; the second is relative, always changing in response to the increase or refinement of knowledge. The two series correspond more or less, it is our aim to make the correspondence as exact as possible; but the actual series of events exists for us only in terms of the ideal series which we affirm and hold in memory." "Everyman His Own Historian" (1931), *Everyman*, p. 234. I have discussed the differences between Becker's views and those of Common Sense philosophy in "J. Gresham Machen, History, and Truth," *Westminster Theological Journal*, 42 (1979), 157–175.

8. "Postscript," *Structure*, p. 206. Hayden White, drawing upon literary theory, comes to similar conclusions as to the dominant role of the subjective in historical narrative. He writes: "Histories, then, are not only about events but also about the possible sets of relationships that those events can be demonstrated to figure. These sets or relationships are not, however, immanent in the events themselves; they exist only in the mind of the historian reflecting on them." "The Historical Text as Literary Artifact," Robert H. Canary and Henry Kozlicki, eds., *The Writing of History* (Madison, 1978), p. 55.

9. A major exception is Wolfhart Pannenberg, who reacts strongly to this trend and goes to an opposite extreme, claiming that only the events (and not the biblical interpretations of them) have significance.

10. This latter suggestion is the main, though not the only, emphasis of

Nicholas Wolterstorff's *Reason Within the Bounds of Religion* (Grand Rapids, 1976). Wolterstorff's suggestion is a helpful and practical one, so far as it goes.

11. These are discussed in S. A. Grave, *The Scottish Philosophy of Common Sense* (Oxford, 1960), pp. 183–189.

12. From Daniel N. Robinson, "Thomas Reid's *Gestalt* Psychology," in Stephen F. Barker and Tom L. Beauchamp, eds., *Thomas Reid: Critical Interpretations* (Philadelphia, 1976), p. 49.

I see the Gestalt theories of perception as providing important analogies and clues to our abilities for knowing generally. I do not want to press any of the details of Gestalt theory—in fact, I could not press such details if I wanted to, since I am unfamiliar with them.

13. *Dynamics of Spiritual Life: An Evangelical Theology of Renewal* (Downers Grove, Ill., 1979).

14. Donald Mackay, *Human Science and Human Dignity* (Downers Grove, Ill., 1979), p. 29. Mackay's works include helpful suggestions about shifts from one level to another in viewing reality.

Chapter 5   M. Howard Rienstra

1. Roger Trigg, *Reason and Commitment* (New York: Cambridge University Press, 1973), p. 168.

2. "The Baconian fallacy consists in the idea that a historian can operate without the aid of preconceived questions, hypotheses, ideas, assumptions, theories, paradigms, postulates, prejudices, presumptions, or general presuppositions of any kind. He is supposed to go a-wandering in the dark forest of the past, gathering facts like nuts and berries, until he has enough to make a general truth." David H. Fischer, *Historians' Fallacies* (New York: Harper and Row, 1970), p. 4.

3. The best easily accessible introduction to these matters is to be found in W. H. Walsh, *An Introduction to the Philosophy of History* (London: Hutchinson, 1951), pp. 83–90 (also available in Harper Torchbook edition). A competent analysis of Walsh from a specifically Christian point of view is given in a paper by A. N. S. Lane of London Bible College, "Historical Relativism and Biblical Authority," published by the Graduates' Fellowship, 39 Bedford Sq., London, under the title *Christianity and Historical Relativism,* 1973.

4. J. A. Passmore, "The Objectivity of History," in W. H. Dray, ed., *Philosophical Analysis and History* (New York: Harper and Row, 1966), pp. 76–89.

5. Israel Scheffler, *Science and Subjectivity* (New York: Bobbs-Merrill, 1967), p. 114.

6. Nicholas Wolterstorff, *Reason Within the Bounds of Religion* (Grand Rapids: Eerdmans, 1976), *passim.*

7. Quoted in Moses I. Finley, *The Use and Abuse of History* (New York: Viking Press, 1971), p. 11.

8. There is a vast literature about historical explanation that continues to appear in the journal *History and Theory* and in several journals in the philosophy of science. Two convenient anthologies are the previously cited one by Dray, *Philosophical Analysis and History,* and one edited by Patrick Gardiner, *Theories of History* (New York: The Free Press, 1959).

9. See particularly Hayden V. White, "The Burden of History," *History and Theory,* 5 (1966), 111–134.

10. Fritz Medicus, "The Objectivity of Historical Knowledge," in R. Klibansky and H. J. Paton, eds., *Philosophy and History: The Ernst Cassirer Festschrift* (New York: Harper and Row, 1963), p. 149.

11. *Ibid.,* p. 147.

12. Charles Crowe, "Slavery, Ideology and Cliometrics" (review article), *Technology and Culture,* 17 (1976), 271–285.

13. Thomas S. Kuhn, *The Copernican Revolution* (Cambridge: Harvard University Press, 1959). Also available as a Modern Library paperback.

14. Thomas S. Kuhn, *The Structure of Scientific Revolutions* (Chicago: University of Chicago Press, 1962).

15. Wolterstorff, *Reason,* p. 24.

16. *Ibid.,* p. 25.

17. *Ibid.,* p. 63.

18. *Ibid.,* p. 64.

19. *Ibid.,* pp. 70–71.

20. William J. Bouwsma, "Christian Adulthood," *Daedalus* (Spring, 1976), 77.

21. Wolterstorff, *Reason,* p. 72.

22. Maurice Mandelbaum, *The Anatomy of Historical Knowledge* (Baltimore: The Johns Hopkins University Press, 1977), p. 150.

Chapter 6   Robert T. Handy

1. "Theodosius' Horse: Reflections on the Predicament of the Church Historian," *Church History,* 34 (1965), 253.

2. "Many Mansions," *American Historical Review,* 59 (1963–1964), 315.

3. *Friedrich Heinrich Jacobi's auserlesener Briefwechsel* (Leipzig, 1827), II, 478, as cited by Martin E. Marty, *The Modern Schism: Three Paths to the Secular* (New York: Harper & Row, 1969), p. 41.

4. *The Historian and the Believer: The Morality of Historical Knowledge and Christian Belief* (New York: Macmillan Co., 1966), pp. 14, 38, 103.

5. *Professor Rauschenbusch's "Christianity and the Social Crisis"* (New York: Charles C. Cook, n.d. [1912?]), p. 41.

6. *Christian Thought: Its History and Application* (New York: Meridian Books, 1957), p. 37.

7. *The Faith of Modernism* (New York: Macmillan Co., 1924), pp. 23–35.

8. *Church Dogmatics,* IV, *The Doctrine of Reconciliation,* Part I (Edinburgh: T. & T. Clark, 1956), 657.

9. *The Secularization of the European Mind in the Nineteenth Century* (Cambridge: Cambridge University Press, 1975), p. 192.

10. *Tradition and the Modern World: Reformed Theology in the Nineteenth Century* (Chicago: University of Chicago Press, 1977), p. x.

11. *The Meaning of Revelation* (New York: Macmillan Co., 1941), pp. 173–174.

12. II Cor. 5:18–19.

13. Hoskyns and Noel Davey, *The Riddle of the New Testament* (London: Faber & Faber, 1931), p. 10.

14. "The Seminary in the Ecumenical Age," *Princeton Seminary Bulletin,* 54 (1960), 41.

15. *Christianity and History* (London: G. Bell & Sons, 1949), p. 107.

16. "Metaphysics and the Problem of Historicism in Contemporary Theology," in Paul L. Williams, ed., *Historicism and Faith* (Scranton: Northeast Books, 1980), p. 99

17. "History as a Social Science: A Christian's Response," in George Marsden and Frank Roberts, eds., *A Christian View of History?* (Grand Rapids: Eerdmans, 1975), p. 96.

18. *The Historian and the Believer*, p. 283.

Chapter 7   Robert P. Swierenga

1. Thomas S. Kuhn, *The Structure of Scientific Revolutions* (Chicago: University of Chicago Press, 1962), and more recently Kuhn's *The Essential Tension: Selected Studies in Scientific Tradition and Change* (Chicago: University of Chicago Press, 1979). For a perceptive Kuhnian analysis of the sociology discipline, see George Ritzer, *Sociology, A Multiple Paradigm Science* (Boston, 1975).

2. Robert P. Swierenga, "Computers and American History: The Impact of the 'New' Generation," *Journal of American History*, 60 (1974), 1045–1070, esp. 1052–1061; Robert P. Swierenga, ed., *Quantification in American History: Theory and Research* (New York: Atheneum, 1970), pp. xi–xxi. See also the citations in note 3.

3. George G. S. Murphy, "The 'New' History," *Explorations in Entrepreneurial History*, 2 (1965), 132–146; Gertrude Himmelfarb, "The 'New History,'" *Commentary* (Jan. 1975), 72–78; "The New History: the 1980s and Beyond," a series of 17 articles in two successive issues of the *Journal of Interdisciplinary History*, 12 (Summer, Autumn 1981); Jerome M. Clubb and Allan G. Bogue, "History, Quantification and the Social Science," *American Behavioral Scientist*, 21 (1977), 167–185; Lawrence Stone, "The Revival of Narrative History: Reflections on a New Old History," *Past and Present*, 85 (1979), 3–24.

4. A listing of key journals includes: *Historical Methods, Journal of Interdisciplinary History, Journal of Social History, Computers and the Humanities, Journal of Family History, Journal of Urban History, Journal of American Ethnic History, Journal of Psychohistory, Journal of Historical Geography, Peasant History Newsletter, History of Childhood Quarterly*. An analysis of "quantitative" articles appearing in five leading historical journals since 1961 is J. Morgan Kousser, "Quantitative Social-Scientific History," in Michael Kammen, ed., *The Past Before Us* (Ithaca, N.Y.: Cornell University Press), pp. 433–456.

5. David Landes and Charles Tilly, eds., *History as Social Science* (Englewood Cliffs, N.J.: Prentice-Hall, 1971), pp. 5–21.

6. Frederick Adams Woods, "Historiometry," *Science*, 30 (1909), 703–704.

7. Jacques Barzun, *Clio and the Doctors: Psycho-History, Quanto-History, and History* (Chicago: University of Chicago Press, 1974).

8. "Toward an Intelligence Beyond Man's," *Time*, Feb. 20, 1978, p. 59.

9. Swierenga, *Quantification in American History*, xii–xiv. An essay that links the new history of the 1900–1920 era to the social scientific history of the 1960–1980 era is David L. Gross, "The 'New History' and Beyond: The View from the 1970's," *Social Science Journal*, 15 (1980), 23–38.

10. Quoted in Swierenga, *Quantification in American History*, xiii.

11. I am relying in this paragraph and the next on Lawrence Stone, "History and the Social Sciences in the Twentieth Century," in Charles F. Delzell, ed., *The Future of History* (Nashville: Vanderbilt University Press, 1977), pp. 3–42,

esp. pp. 6–12. See also Social Science Research Council, *Theory and Practice in Historical Study: A Report of the Committee on Historiography, Bulletin 54, 1946* (New York: Social Science Research Council, 1946); and *The Social Sciences in Historical Study: A Report of the Committee on Historiography, Bulletin 64, 1954* (New York: Social Science Research Council, 1954). For an excellent discussion of the impact of the Bulletins, see John Higham, with Leonard Krueger and Felix Gilbert, *History: The Development of Historical Studies in the United States* (Englewood Cliffs, N.J.: Prentice-Hall, 1965), pp. 129–140.

12. Samuel P. Hays, "History as Human Behavior," *Iowa Journal of History*, 58 (1960), 193–206 (the quotes are on p. 193). Hays carried this same message to the Organization of American Historians in 1973. See "History and the Changing University Curriculum," *The History Teacher*, 8 (1974), 64–72.

13. Bruce M. Stave, "A Conversation with Samuel P. Hays," *Journal of Urban History*, 2 (1975), 88–124, esp. 96. All of Hays's major essays are collected in Samuel P. Hays, ed., *American Political History As Social Analysis* (Knoxville: University of Tennessee Press, 1980). Hays's introductory essay is especially valuable for tracing the development of his thinking (pp. 3–45).

14. Aydelotte's seminal work is collected in his edited book, *Quantification in History* (Reading, Mass.: Addison Wesley, 1971), chaps. 4–5. See also William O. Aydelotte, Allan G. Bogue, Robert William Fogel, eds., *The Dimensions of Quantitative Research in History* (Princeton: Princeton University Press, 1972). Bogue's research culminated in *From Prairie to Corn Belt: Farming on the Illinois and Iowa Prairies in the Nineteenth Century* (Chicago: University of Chicago Press, 1963) and *The Ernest Men: Republicans in the Civil War Senate* (Ithaca and London: Cornell University Press, 1981). The development of the so-called Iowa School is described in William Silag, "Pioneers in Quantitative History at the University of Iowa," *Annals of Iowa*, 46 (1981), 121–134, but this article must be used with caution.

15. William O. Aydelotte, "Quantification in History," *American Historical Review*, 71 (1966), 803–825, reprinted in Aydelotte, *Quantification in History*, pp. 39–65. Also essential is Aydelotte's "Introduction," pp. 1–38. Allan Bogue's views are summarized in "Numerical and Formal Analysis in United States History," *Journal of Interdisciplinary History*, 12 (1981), 137–175.

16. *Quantification in History*, pp. 40, 41, 60, 35.

17. The report is reprinted in Lee Benson, *Toward the Scientific Study of History: Selected Essays* (Philadelphia: J. B. Lippencott, 1972), pp. 3–80.

18. *Ibid.*, p. 10. An excellent exposition of the implications of such a question is Robert F. Berkhofer, Jr., *A Behavioral Approach to Historical Analysis* (New York: Free Press, 1969), pp. 270–291, esp. pp. 284–285.

19. Benson's influence is traced in Bogue, "Numerical and Formal Analysis," 162–166.

20. Lee Benson, "Quantification, Scientific History, and Scholarly Analysis," *American Historical Association Newsletter*, 4 (1966), 11–16, reprinted in Benson, *Scientific Study of History*, pp. 98–104, and in Swierenga, *Quantification in American History*, pp. 25–29. The fact that Benson is enamored of Buckle, one of the leading European scientific historians of the last century, suggests that, in one sense, Benson is not avant-garde. He wants to restore to the history classroom the commitment to "scientific" thinking and outside the classroom the commitment to solving immediate political problems by applying a mixture of scientific analysis and human compassion. See Deborah L. Haines, "Scientific History as

a Teaching Method: The Formative Years," *Journal of American History*, 63 (1977), 892–912, esp. 895, 902; Higham, *History*, pp. 6–25, 92–103, 147–170, and citations in Haines, 892, n. 1. An excellent summary and critique of Buckle's views is Gordon H. Clark, *Historiography: Secular and Religious* (Nutley, N.J.: Craig Press, 1971), Chapter 3, "Statistical Law," pp. 57–71.

21. Stave, "Conversation with Samuel P.- Hays," 109–110; Peter Laslett, "History and the Social Sciences," *International Encyclopedia of the Social Sciences* (6 vols.; New York: Macmillan, 1968), VI, 437–438.

22. For example, see Ralph Mann, "Science and Polemics: Lee Benson and History," *The Historian*, 35 (1972), 92–93.

23. Morton Rothstein, Samuel T. McSeveney, Philip J. Greven, Jr., Robert Zemsky, and Joel Silbey, "Quantification and American History: An Assessment," in Herbert J. Bass, ed., *The State of American History* (Chicago: Quadrangle Books, 1970), p. 316.

24. Sheldon Hackney, "Power to the Computers: A Revolution in History?" AFIPS Spring Joint Computer Conference *Proceedings*, 36 (1970), 275–277.

25. Robert William Fogel, "The Limits of Quantitative Methods in History," *American Historical Review*, 80 (1975), 329–350. However, Fogel's controversial book (with Stanley L. Engerman), *Time on the Cross: The Economics of American Negro Slavery* (Boston: Little Brown, 1974), which treats facts as "neutral," seems to belie his denial of objective truth.

26. The best analyses are David A. Hollinger, "T. S. Kuhn's Theory of Science and Its Implications for History," *American Historical Review*, 78 (1973), 370–393; and David Ricci, "Reading Thomas Kuhn in the Post-Behavioral Era," *Western Political Quarterly*, 30 (1977), 7–34.

27. An excellent brief statement is Ricci, "Reading Thomas Kuhn." A more extended discussion by a gifted historian is Berkhofer, *Behavioral Approach to Historical Analysis*.

28. Robert W. Fogel, "Circumstantial Evidence in 'Scientific' and Traditional History," in David Carr et al., eds., *Philosophy of History and Contemporary Historiography* (Ottawa: University of Ottawa Press, 1982), pp. 61–112; D. J. Bartholomew, "Probability and Social Science," *International Social Science Journal*, 27 (1975), 419–436.

29. Aydelotte, *Quantification in History*, p. 29.

30. Quoted in Ricci, "Reading Thomas Kuhn," 11.

31. David Wolfe, "Theoretical Pluralism and the Dreams of Childhood: An Immoderate Proposal for Christian Sociologists," paper presented to the Institute for Advanced Christian Studies Conference, Wheaton, Ill., 1978, p. 5.

32. Quoted in Ricci, "Reading Thomas Kuhn," 12.

33. Daniel J. Boorstin, *America and the Image of Europe, Reflections on American Thought* (New York, 1960), p. 66.

34. Barzun stridently stated the case for this position in *Clio and the Doctors*, and in "History: The Muse and Her Doctors," *American Historical Review*, 77 (1972), 36–64. See also Carl Bridenbaugh, "The Great Mutation," *American Historical Review*, 68 (1963), 315–331; Oscar Handlin, "History—A Discipline in Crisis," *The American Scholar*, 40 (1971), and Oscar Handlin, "The Capacity of Quantitative History," *Perspectives in American History*, 9 (1975), 7–26.

35. Jack H. Hexter, "The Rhetoric of History," *International Encyclopedia of the Social Sciences*, VI, 368–394. Hexter expanded on this and other criticisms in *The History Primer* (New York, 1970) and in *Doing History* (Bloomington: Univer-

sity of Indiana Press, 1971). Aydelotte's reasoned reply to Hexter is in his *Quantification in History*, pp. 155–179, esp. p. 159.

36. Ritzer, *Sociology*, p. 18.

37. Gary M. Fink and James W. Hilty, "Prologue: The Senate Voting Record of Harry S. Truman," *Journal of Interdisciplinary History*, 55 (1973), 207–235.

38. Kenneth Lockridge, "Historical Demography," in Delzell, *Future of History*, p. 61. A similar attack on the presumed "neutral facts" syndrome is Stephen L. Hansen, "The Illusion of Objectivism: A Review of Recent Trends in the New Political History," *Historical Methods*, 12 (1979), 105–110.

39. H. Van Riessen, *The Society of the Future* (Philadelphia, 1952), p. 127.

40. Theodore Rottman, "A Christian View of Sociology," in William Smith, ed., *Christian Perpsectives in Sociology* (Grand Rapids, 1978), pp. 2, 6.

41. Lawrence Stone, "History and the Social Sciences," 38–39. Liam Hudson, *The Cult of the Fact: A Psychologist's Autobiographical Critique of his Discipline* (New York, 1972), p. 155.

42. Bernard Zylstra, "Sabbatical Research in Political Theory 1976–1977," *Perspective*, 11 (1977), 8.

43. Lockridge, "Historical Demography," 61.

44. *Ibid.*, 62.

45. Barzun, *Clio and the Doctors*, pp. 82, 61–62, and *passim*.

46. Himmelfarb, "New History," 77.

47. Lee Benson, "Changing Social History to Change the World: A Discussion Paper," *Social Science History*, 2 (1978), 427–441 (the quotes are on p. 427). An expanded version of Benson's neo-Marxist agenda is discussed in "Doing History as Moral Philosophy and Public Advocacy: A Practical Strategy to Lessen the Crisis in American History," paper presented to the Organization of American Historians, Detroit, April 1, 1981. A similar mission is stated in Duncan MacRae, Jr., *The Social Function of Social Science* (New Haven: Yale University Press, 1976). A Christian critique of this belief in science and technique is Van Riessen, *Society of the Future*, esp. pp. 117–164. For a conservative critique, see John Caiazza, "Analyzing the Social 'Scientist,'" *The Intercollegiate Review*, 16 (1981), 91–98.

48. Benson, *Scientific Study of History*, pp. 327–333 (the quote is on p. 331).

49. *Ibid.*, pp. 327–328 (all italics are the author's).

50. For conservative critique along these lines, see Thomas Molnar, "Ethnology and Environmentalism: Man as Animal and Mechanism," *The Intercollegiate Review*, 13 (1977), 25–43; John C. Caiazza, "Modern Science and the Origins of Our Political discontent," *ibid.*, 15–24; Aileen S. Kraditor, "On Curiosity: or, the Difference Between an Ideologue and a Scholar," *The Intercollegiate Review*, 15 (1980), 95–99.

51. Aydelotte, "Lee Benson's Scientific History: For and Against," *Journal of Interdisciplinary History*, 4 (1973), 271.

52. Robert W. Fogel, "'Scientific' History and Traditional History," in L. J. Cohen, J. Los, H. Pfieffer, and K.-P. Podewski, eds., *Logic, Methodology and Philosophy of Science*, VI.

53. So, for example, Earle E. Cairns, *God and Man in Time: A Christian Approach to Historiography* (Grand Rapids: Baker, 1979), pp. 20-23.

54. Two excellent studies, one in history and one in psychology, that explain these traditions in a sympathetic, yet critical, manner and link them to a

Christian base are David W. Bebbington, *Patterns in History: A Christian View* (Downers Grove, Ill.: InterVarsity Press, 1979); and C. Stephen Evans, *Preserving the Person: A Look at the Human Sciences* (Downers Grove, Ill.: InterVarsity Press, 1977).

55. Rottman, "Christian View," 1, 99 n. 1; Richard J. Mouw, "Some Guidelines for the Christian Study of Man," *Christianity Today*, March 1973, 22–24; Richard H. Bube, "Science and pseudoscience," *The Reformed Journal*, Nov. 1982, 10–13.

56. Several creative attempts are Wolfe, "Theoretical Pluralism"; Richard J. Mouw, "Explaining Social Reality: Some Christian Reflections" (paper presented to the Institute for Advanced Christian Studies, Wheaton College, 1977); and Dale Dannefer's response, "Some Reflections on Richard Mouw's 'Reflections,'" presented at the same conference; Jack Balswick and Dawn War, "The Nature of Man and Scientific Models of Society," *Journal of the American Scientific Affiliation*, 28 (1976), 181–185; Mark A. Noll, "Scientific History in America: a Centennial Observation from a Christian Point of View" (paper presented at the Conference on Faith and History, Chicago, September 25, 1980).

Chapter 8   Dale Van Kley

1. On the French Catholic Church, see Pierre de la Gorce, *Histoire religieuse de la révolution française* (5 vols.; Paris, 1902–1903); Albert Mathiez, *Le révolution et l'église* (Paris, 1910); Alphonse Aulard, *Le christianisme et la révolution française* (Paris, 1924); André Latreille, *L'église catholique et la révolution française* (2 vols.; Paris, 1946–1950), probably the best narrative account; and more recently John McManners, *The French Revolution and the Church* (New York and Evanston, 1969); Bernard Plongeron, *Conscience religieuse et révolution: regards sur l'historiographie religieuse de la révolution française* (Paris, 1969) and *Théologie et politique au siècle des lumières, 1770–1820* (Geneva, 1973). For the Protestant churches, see Burdette C. Poland, *French Protestantism and the Revolution* (Princeton, 1957). Michel Vovelle's recent *Religion et révolution: la déchristianisation de l'an II* (Paris, 1976) concerns both Catholics and Protestants, but is somewhat narrow and technical in nature.

2. The image of man briefly sketched here owes most to Reinhold Niebuhr, *The Nature and Destiny of Man* (2 vols.; New York, 1964), I, *Human Nature*, esp. pp. 13–18; and Blaise Pascal, *Pensées*, in *Oeuvres complètes*, Louis Lafuma, ed. (New York, 1963), esp. sections VI (grandeur) and VII (contrariétés), pp. 512–516.

3. For an example of said denigration, chosen entirely at random, see David N. Pinkney's review of James K. Kieswetter's *Etienne-Denis Pasquier: The Last Chancellor of France*, in the *American Historical Review*, 82 (1977), 1266. Pinkney here castigates Kieswetter's book for being mere political history, which in turn he defines as "the frothy surface of history." This metaphor to describe political history goes back to Fernand Braudel, *La mediterranée et le monde mediterranéen à l'époque de Philippe II* (2nd ed.; 2 vols; Paris, 1966), I, 16, as does the phrase "longue durée," *ibid.*, 21. As is often the case, the master was more generous toward the historiographical tradition from which he was departing than were his more niggardly and dogmatic disciples. Although he thought that "histoire événementielle" was "dangereux" because its very noise and movement

risked creating a false sense of importance, he acknowledged that it was also "la plus passionnante, la plus riche en humanité. . . . " (*ibid.*, 16).

4. Georges Lefebvre, *The Coming of the French Revolution*, trans. R. R. Palmer (Princeton, 1871), pp. 1–2, or Albert Soboul, *Les sans-culottes parisiens en l'an II: mouvement populaire et gouvernement révolutionnaire, 2 juin 1793 à thermidore an II* (Paris, 1958), *passim*. In the first sentence of this monumental *thèse*, Soboul states his basic premise: "The French Revolution, along with the English revolutions of the seventeenth century, constitute the culmination of a long economic and social revolution that made the middle classes masters of the world" (*ibid.*, 1).

5. On the social and political aspects of the thesis of "aristocratic revolution," see Elinore Barber, *The Bourgeoisie in Eighteenth-Century France* (Princeton, 1955); Franklin L. Ford, *Robe and Sword: The Regrouping of the French Aristocracy after Louis XIV* (Cambridge, Mass., 1962); and Robert R. Palmer, *The Age of the Democratic Revolution: A Political History of Europe and America, 1760–1800* (2 vols.; Princeton, 1959–1964), I, *The Challenge* (1959), *passim*, but esp. 41–44, 73–74, 86–99, 349–465. The idea can also be found in the works of Marxist historians, for example Lefebvre, *The Coming*, the section subtitled "The Resurgence of the Aristocracy in the Eighteenth Century," pp. 15–20, or Albert Soboul, *Histoire de la révolution française* (2 vols.; Paris, 1962), I, *De la Bastille à la Gironde*, 29–30.

6. On the rural aspect of "aristocratic reaction," see Lefebvre, *The Coming*, pp. 14, 140–142, as well as his "La révolution française et les paysans," in *Etudes sur la révolution française* (Paris, 1963), pp. 150–153. See also Alan Davies, "The Origins of the French Peasant Revolution of 1789," *History*, new ser., 49 (1964), 24–41, but esp. 35–37; and Robert Forster, *The Nobility in Toulouse in the Eighteenth Century: A Social and Economic Study* (Baltimore, 1960), pp. 49–53. Even Alfred Cobban, who debunks so much, lends a certain credence to this thesis in *The Social Interpretation of the French Revolution* (Cambridge, 1964), pp. 36–53.

7. The relationship between the sociological school of "functionalism" and the thesis of aristocratic reaction is quite explicit. The dustjacket of Elinore Barber's *The Bourgeoisie in Eighteenth-Century France* quotes R. R. Palmer, in the *Political Science Quarterly*, to the effect that "Mrs. Barber applies to the eighteenth century in France certain concepts formulated in the sociology of Talcott Parsons and Robert K. Merton. . . ."

8. Besides Cobban, *The Social Interpretation*, pp. 25–35, see also Marc Bloch, *French Rural History: An Essay on its Basic Characteristics*, Janet Sondheimer, trans. (Berkeley, 1966), pp. 102–149.

9. Cobban, *The Social Interpretation*, *passim*. The following sentence (p. 53) sums up his work of destruction: "The abolition of seigneurial dues was the work of the peasantry, unwillingly accepted by the men who drew up the town and *bailliage cahiers*, and forced on the National Assembly through the fear inspired by a peasant revolt. It follows that the 'overthrow of feudalism by the bourgeoisie' takes on very much the appearance of the myth I suggested it was in a lecture some eight years ago." The reference is to his "The Myth of the French Revolution," now published in *Aspects of the French Revolution* (New York, 1970), pp. 99–104.

10. In fact, Cobban makes no contribution to this important point. See, rather, Pierre Goubert, *L'ancien régime* (2 vols.; Paris, 1969–1972), I, *La Société* (1969), 232–235. For the socially heterogeneous nature of the world of finance, see Herbert Luthy, *La banque protestante en France de l'édit de Nantes à la révolution*

(2 vols.; Paris, 1959–1961); Yves Durand, *Les fermiers généraux au XVIIIe siècle* (Paris, 1971). Guy Chaussinand-Nogaret, *Gens de finance de Languédoc au XVIIIe siècle de la féodalité aux lumières* (Paris, 1976), came to my attention too late to impinge upon the argument of this paper.

11. Cobban, "The Myth of the French Revolution," 99–104.

12. George V. Taylor, "Types of Capitalism in Eighteenth-Century France," *English Historical Review,* 79 (1964), 478–497, and "Non-Capitalistic Wealth and the Origins of the French Revolution," *American Historical Review,* 72 (1967), 469–496.

13. On definitions and theory, see Max Weber, "Class, Status and Party," in Gerth and Mills, eds., *From Max Weber: Essays in Sociology* (New York, 1946), pp. 180–195.

14. On the ubiquity of privilege, see Goubert, *L'ancien régime,* I, *passim,* but esp. ch. VII, 45–159; C.B.A. Behrens, "Nobles, Privileges and Taxes in France at the End of the Ancien Régime," *Economic History Review,* 2nd series, 15 (1963), 451–475; and Jeffrey Kaplow, *The Names of Kings: The Parisian Laboring Poor in the Eighteenth Century* (New York, 1972), esp. pp. 27–65, which document numbers of cases of petty privileges among the Parisian *menu peuple.* For the pervasiveness of privilege in the publishing world, see Robert Darnton, "The High Enlightenment and the Low Life of Literature in Pre-Revolutionary France," *Past and Present,* 51 (1971), 81–115, recently reprinted in Douglas Johnson, ed., *French Society and The Revolution* (Cambridge, 1976), pp. 53–87.

15. This is the general picture that emerges from Goubert's *L'ancien régime,* I. See also Colin Lucas, "Nobles, Bourgeois and the Origins of the French Revolution," *Past and Present,* no. 60 (August 1973), 84–126, and reprinted in Douglas Johnson, *French Society,* pp. 91–92.

16. Vivien Gruder, *The Royal Provincial Intendants: A Governing Elite in Eighteenth-Century France* (Ithaca, 1968), esp. pp. 167–207.

17. David D. Bien, "La réaction aristocratique avant 1789: l'example de l'armée," J. Rovet, trans., *Annales Economies Sociétés Civilisations,* 29 année (1974), 23–48, 505–534. Unfortunately, this article is nowhere published in English, even though originally written in that language. For a more general attack on "aristocratic reaction," see William Doyle, "Was There an Aristocratic Reaction in Pre-Revolutionary France?" *Past and Present,* 57 (1972), 97–122, and republished in Johnson, *French Society,* pp. 3–27. This article also subjects the rural dimension of the thesis to destructive scrutiny. Jean Egret's "L'aristocratie parlementaire à la fin de l'ancien régime," *Revue historique,* 208 (1952), 1–14, although sometimes cited in support of the thesis of aristocratic reaction, is in reality quite destructive of it.

18. Thomas Kuhn, *The Structure of Scientific Revolutions* (2nd ed.; Chicago, 1970), esp. pp. 77–91.

19. François Furet, "Le catéchisme de la révolution française," *Annales E. S. C.,* 26 année (1971), 255–289, but esp. 268. This article has recently been translated and published in Ralph W. Greenlaw, ed., *The Social Origins of the French Revolution: The Debate on the Role of the Middle Classes* (Lexington, Toronto, and London: Heath problems series, 1975), pp. 61–97.

20. It is possible that the sociological theory of "status anxiety" is relevant to the present case. See Laurence Stone's discussion of this theory in the context of the English Civil War in Forster and Green, eds., *Preconditions of Revolution in Early Modern Europe,* p. 62, as well as the statement of the theory by Gerhard E.

Lenski, "Status Crystallization: a Non-Vertical Dimension of Social Status," *The American Sociological Review*, 19 (1954), 405–413.

21. Alexis de Tocqueville, *The Old Regime and the French Revolution*, Stuart Gilbert, trans. (Garden City, New York, 1955), in general pp. 77–96, in particular pp. 89, 96.

22. For an eloquent example of how this was done, see David D. Bien, "The Secrétaires du Roi: Absolutism, Corporatism, and Privilege under the ancien Régime," in Ernst Hinrichs, Eberhad Schmitt, and Rudoff Vierhaus, eds., *De l'ancien régime à la révolution française* (Göttingen, 1978), pp. 153–168. For de Tocqueville on the state, *Old Regime*, 14–76.

23. *Ibid.*, 137.

24. For example, Goubert, *L'ancien régime*, I, 12–16; Furet, "Le catéchisme de la révolution française," 269, and "Tocqueville et le problème de la Révolution française," in *Penser la révolution française* (Paris, 1978), pp. 173–211; Bien, "The Secrétaires du Roi," 168; and Soboul, *La civilization et la révolution française* (2 vols.; Paris, 1970), I, *La crise de l'ancien régime*, 64. Darnton's "The High Enlightenment and the Low-Life of Literature," although it nowhere cites Tocqueville, seems everywhere close to his thought.

25. Doris S. Goldstein, *Trial of Faith: Religion and Politics in Tocqueville's Thought* (New York, 1975), *passim*.

26. François Furet underscores this point in his recent *Penser la révolution française*, esp. pp. 22–23, 27–28, 33–35, 41.

27. George V. Taylor, "Non-Capitalistic Wealth and the Origins of the French Revolution," 495–496, has similarly insisted on the radicalizing significance of this event.

28. Furet, *Penser la révolution française*, *passim*. But on p. 39 he states his position succinctly: "En d'autres termes, le débat sur les causes de la Révolution ne recouvre pas le problème révolutionnaire, largement indépendant de la situation qui prècéde: développant lui-même ses propres conséquences. Ce qui caractérise la Révolution comme événement, c'est une modalité de l'action historique; c'est une dynamique qu'on pourra appeler politique, idéologique ou culturelle, pour dire que son pouvoir multiplié de mobilisation des hommes et d'action sur les choses passe par un surinvestissement de sens."

29. For a recent confirmation of this trend, although in another field, see the discussion of the origins of the English Civil War by Gruenfelder, Christianson, Roberts, Kishlansky, and Farnell in *Journal of Modern History*, 49 (1977), 557–660. These revisionist articles have this much in common, that they all represent a return to political history and contend that an understanding of the English Civil War without reference to politics is no understanding of it at all. In the following issue of the same journal, 50 (1978), Jack Hexter acknowledges that this much represents progress, but argues, as does this essay, that it does not go far enough, that politics is at least sometimes about more than just the workings of institutions and the pursuit of power. More recently still, Keith Michael Baker, in "Enlightenment and Revolution in France: Old Problems, Renewed Approaches," *Journal of Modern History*, 53 (1981), 281–303, has underscored the need "to rediscover the politics of the last decades of the Old Regime."

30. Edmund Burke, *Reflections on the Revolution in France*, Thomas Mahoney, ed. (Indianapolis and New York, 1955), *passim;* and Augustin de Barruel, *Mémoires pour servir à l'histoire du jacobinisme* (Lyons, 1818–1819), *passim.*

31. Hughes Félicité de Lamennais, *Influence des doctrines philosophiques sur*

la société in *Oeuvres complétes* (12 vols.; Paris, 1836–1837), VI, *passim.* On 119, he draws the connection between the "novateurs du seizième siècle" and the philosophes. See also Joseph-Marie comte de Maistre, esp. his *Study on Sovereignty,* section reprinted in William F. Church, ed., *The Influence of the Enlightenment on the French Revolution* (2nd ed.; Lexington, Toronto, and London, 1974), pp. 32–38. Among Napoleonic and Restoration authors, Barruel most strenuously insisted upon the conspiratorial nature of the philosophers' influence, but his argument has not failed to elicit an "amen" or two from the moderns, notably Augustin Cochin, *Les sociétés de pensée et la démocratie* (Paris, 1921), *passim;* and Pierre Gaxotte, member of the French Academy, *The French Revolution,* Walter A. Phillips, trans. (New York, 1932), esp. pp. 40–41, 49–52.

32. Guillaume Groen van Prinsterer, *Ongeloof en revolutie: eene reeks van historische voorlezingen* (Leiden, 1847); and *Le parti anti-révolutionaaire et confessionel dan l'eglise réformée des pays-bas* (Amsterdam, 1860).

33. Thomas Paine, *The Rights of Man,* in Philip S. Foner, ed., *The Complete Writings of Thomas Paine* (2 vols.; New York, 1945), I, 259–272, 298–313.

34. I voluntarily confound the liberal and republican traditions in France. Distinct enough under the Restoration and the July monarchy, the former was pretty much absorbed by the latter thereafter. For a Third Republic republican, see François Victor Alphonse Aulard, *The French Revolution: A Political History* (4 vols.; New York, 1965), I, 79–126. For the liberals properly speaking, see Adolphe Thiers, *The History of the French Revolution,* F. Shroberl, trans. (4 vols.; New York, 1882), I, 15–193; and F. A. Mignet, *History of the French Revolution from 1789 to 1814* (London, 1891), pp. 1–97. Thiers and Mignet were both Restoration liberals, that is constitutional monarchists, who published their respective histories at about the same time—Thiers between 1823 and 1827, Mignet in 1824. For partial confirmation of my characterization of the "liberal" historiographical tradition's attitude toward the Enlightenment, see Paul Farmer, *France Reviews its Revolutionary Origins* (New York, 1963), p. 40.

35. Daniel Mornet, *Les origines intellectuelles de la révolution française* (6th ed.; Paris, 1967), p. 3.

36. The phrase was coined by Peter Gay, *The Party of Humanity: Essays in the French Revolution* (New York, 1964), p. x. On this subject, see also Robert Darton, "In Search of the Enlightenment: Recent Attempts to Create a Social History of Ideas," *Journal of Modern History,* 43 (1971), 113–137.

37. The "social history of ideas" partly overlaps but is not altogether congruous with what is now called the "histoire des mentalités" which attempts to get below the level of formally expressed ideas to more implicit mental structures and show changes in these on the part of the masses or at least considerable numbers of people. Distinguished examples are Michele Vovelle, *Piété baroque et déchristianisation en Provence au XVIIIe siècle: les attitudes devant la mort d'après les clauses des testaments* (Paris, 1973); and Robert Mandrou, *De la culture populaire aux 17e et 18e siècles: la bibliothèque bleue de Troyes* (n.p.: Stock, 1875).

38. Jacques Proust, *Diderot et l'Encyclopédie* (Paris, 1967), pp. 36–37, and in general pp. 9–43.

39. Robert Darton, "The *Encyclopédie* Wars of Prerevolutionary France," *American Historical Review,* 78 (1973), 1331–1352; and *The Business of Enlightenment: A Publishing History of the Encyclopédie, 1775–1800* (Cambridge, Mass., and London, 1979), pp. 278–299.

40. Daniel Roche, *Le siècle des lumières en province: Académies et academiciens provinciaux, 1660–1789* (2 vols.; Paris and The Hague, 1978), *passim*. For an interpretation of Roche's brute findings, see Keith Baker's magnificent "Enlightenment and Revolution in France: Old Problems, Renewed Approaches," 293–298. See also Roche's earlier "Milieux académiques proviniaux et société des lumières" in François Furet, ed., *Livre et Société dans la France du XVIIIᵉ siècle* (2 vols.; Paris and The Hague, 1965–1970), I, 93–184.

41. Robert Darnton, "The High Enlightenment and the Low Life of Literature"; "The Grub Street Style of Revolution: J.-P. Brissot, Police Spy," *Journal of Modern History*, 40 (1968), 301–327; and "Reading, Writing, and Publishing in Eighteenth-Century France: A Case Study in the Sociology of Literature," *Daedalus* (Winter 1971), 214–256.

42. Darnton, "The High Enlightenment and the Low Life of Literature," 112, 115.

43. Quoted by Jeffrey Kaplow at the 1975 meeting of the French Historical Society in Madison, Wisconsin.

44. By contemporary Frenchmen, I have in view memoirists such as C.-J. F. Barbier, *Chronique de la Régence et du règne de Louis XIV, 1718–1763*, Charpentier, ed. (8 vols.; Paris, 1866); René-Louis d'Argenson, *Journal et mémoires du marquis d'Argenson*, E. J. -B. Rathery, ed. (9 vols.; Paris, 1859–1867); and Mathieu Marais, *Journal et mémoires de Mathieu Marais, avocat au parlement de Paris, sur la régence et le règne de Louis XV, 1715–1737* (4 vols.; Paris, 1803–1808).

45. On Jansenism, secondary works are legion, but the best and most accessible introductions are now probably Louis Cognet, *Le jansénisme* (Paris, 1964); Rene Taveneaux, *Jansénisme et politique* (Paris, 1965); and *Vie quotidienne des jansénistes aux XVIIᵉ et XVIIIᵉ siècles* (Paris, 1973); and in English, Alexander Sedgwick, *Jansenism in 17th-Century France: Voices from the Wilderness* (Charlottesville, Va., 1977). On Gallicanism, see Victor Martin, *Le gallicanisme politique et le clergé de France* (Paris, 1973). On parlementary constitutional thought and rhetoric, see Paul Rice Doolin, *The Fronde* (Cambridge, Mass., 1935); and Rogert Bickart, *Les parlements et la notion de souveraineté nationale au XVIIIᵉ siècle* (Paris, 1932). For an idea of how these elements coalesced, see Van Kley, *The Jansenists and the Expulsion of the Jesuits from France, 1757–1765* (New Haven, 1975), pp. 6–36.

46. Argued by me, *ibid.*, and by Albert Hamscher, "The Parlement of Paris and the Social Interpretation of Early French Jansenism," *Catholic Historical Review*, 63 (1977), 392–410. For the Marxist view, see Lucien Goldmann, *Le dieu caché; étude sur la vision tragique dans les Pensées de Pascal et dans le Théâtre de Racine* (Paris, 1955), *passim*, but esp. 304–314.

47. On *Unigenitus* specifically, see Jacques-François Thomas, *La querelle de l'Unigenitus* (Paris, 1950). See also Jean Egret, *Louis XV et l'opposition parlementaire* (Paris, 1970); Philippe Godard, *La querelle des refus de sacrements, 1730–1765* (Paris, 1937); Georges Hardy, *Le cardinal de Fleury et le mouvement janséniste* (Paris, 1925); and Jacques Parguet, *La bulle Unigenitus et le jansénisme politique* (Paris, 1936). For evidence of the extraordinary persistence, throughout the eighteenth century in France, of the publication of Jansenist theological works among *permissions publiques* and *tacites*, see Furet, "La 'librairie' du royaume de France au XVIIIᵉ siècle," 20, 23.

48. On the character of Jansenist-related movement of political opposition, Van Kley, *Jansenists*, pp. 6–36; and on Jansenist role of expulsion of the

Jesuits, *ibid.*, *passim.* On Jansenist-parlementary victory in the refusal of the sacraments controversy, Van Kley, "The Refusal of the Sacraments Controversy and the Political Crisis of 1756–7 in France," unpublished paper read at the meeting of the ASECS in Chicago, April 1978. What I am suggesting, really, is that the combination of Jansenism, post-1682 Gallicanism, and parlementary constitutionalism produced a movement of political opposition akin to the radical Whiggism which Bernard Bailyn so brilliantly underscores in *The Ideological Origins of the American Revolution* (Cambridge, Mass., 1967).

49. On composition of the *dévôt* or *zélanti parti* within the French episcopacy, see Emile Appolis, *Entre janséniste et zélanti: le 'tiers 'Pierre parti' catholique au XVIII' siècle* (Paris, 1960), 70–109, 217–249, 441–464.

50. For examples of the mid century episcopal rhetoric of persecution, see Regnault, *Christophe de Beaumont archévêque de Paris* (2 vols.; Paris, 1882), especially I, 225–300, which is rich in quotations from the letters of Orleans de la Motte, Bishop of Amiens.

51. On changing episcopal attitudes toward the four Gallican articles, see Norman Ravitch, *Sword and Mitre: Government and Episcopate in France and England in the Age of Aristocracy* (The Hague and Paris, 1966), pp. 20–24. For more direct evidence from primary sources, see Henri-Jacques de Montesquiou, Bishop of Sarlat, *Instruction pastorale de monseigneur l'évêque de Sarlat au clergé séculier et régulier et à tous les fidèles de son diocèse* (Nov. 28, 1764), 15–16; Montmorin de Saint-Herem, Bishop of Langres, *Lettre pastorale de Mgr. l'évêque de Langres au clergé de son diocèse* (Aug. 1, 1763), 8–10; and Lafranc de Pompignan, Bishop of Le Puy, *Défense des Actes du clergé de France, concernant la religion, publiée en l'assemblée de 1765* (Louvain, 1769), pp. 472–473. On episcopal political thought at mid-century, see Van Kley, *Jansenists*, pp. 150–162, which is perhaps applicable to the ultramontanist episcopal group as a whole even though it concerns Jesuit political thought specifically.

52. Stanley Mellon's *The Political Uses of History: A Study of Historians of the French Revolution* (Stanford, Calif., 1958) admirably articulates these divisions as they expressed themselves in the writing of history.

53. D'Argenson, *Journal et mémoires*, 8:313.

54. This cannot be argued in detail here, but for a single example, see Lefranc de Pompignan, *Défense des Actes du clergé de France*, 123–407; and [François Richer], *De l'autorité de clergé et du pouvoir du magistrat politique sur l'exercise des fonctions du ministère écclésiastique. Par M. XXX, avocat au parlement* (2 vols., Amsterdam, 1766), *passim*, but esp. I, 1–27.

55. I have more recently advanced this argument in much more complete form in "Church, State, and the Ideological Origins of the French Revolution: The Debate over the General Assembly of the Gallican Clergy in 1765," *Journal of Modern History,* 51 (1979), 629–666. I argue it even more amply in my book entitled *To Kill a King: The Damiens Affair and the Unravelling of the Old Regime in France, 1750–1770* (Princeton, 1984).

56. Essentially the view of André Latreille, in Latreille and René Rémond, *Histoire du catholicisme en France* (3 vols., Paris, 1957–1962): *La période contemporaine* (1962), 83–94, 96.

57. Perhaps the revolutionary gesture that most eloquently illustrates this association is the "representative on mission" Albitte's campaign, in parts of Southeastern France, to raze all the church steeples and towers which in his opinion excessively lorded it over the surrounding villages and were therefore

too "aristocratic." See Vovelle, *Religion et révolution: la dé-christianisation de l'an II*, p. 170.

    58. For a recent and eloquent illustration of this process, see Timothy Tackett, *Priest and Parish in Eighteenth-Century France: A Social and Political Study of the Curés in a diocese of Dauphiné, 1750–1791* (Princeton, 1977), pp. 249–306.

Index

alienation, 8–9, 12–15, 21
Annales school, 22, 94, 104
Augustine, 8, 24, 42, 52, 53, 66, 67

Becker, Carl, 56–57, 58, 59
belief, 76–81
Benson, Lee, 95–96
Bible, biblical, ix, 3–16, 24, 55, 63, 64, 69
Buckle, Henry, 95
Butterfield, Herbert, 17, 90

change, 27–28
Christian: faith, insights, 8–9, 22, 65, 83–91; interpretation, 13, 103–23; perspective, vii, 30, 55–57, 59–60, 70, 122–23
Cobban, Alfred, 107–10
commitments, 76–82
common sense, 55–68
Creation, the, 11, 35, 87, 90, 99, 103
crisis, vii–x, 8, 17
culture, 3, 11–12, 30–38, 58
culture-making, ix, 20, 30–38, 40
cycles, cyclical, 23–25, 26, 29

destiny, 4–16
determinism, 9, 11, 28, 100
dialectic, 9–10

Enlightenment, 83–86, 113–17, 121–22
epistemology, ix, 55–68, 69–82
event, 3, 23, 113
evil, 9, 14–15, 21, 22. *See* alienation; sin

factors, 35–36, 105–23. *See* multi-factored

fate, 6
freedom, 4–16, 104
French Revolution (1789), ix, 103–23
future, 8, 25–27

Gestalt, 61–62, 64
God: as Creator, 12–14, 35, 66–68, 87, 90, 103; in history, viii, 12–13, 43–44, 51–53, 66–68

historians, viii, 17; Christian, 41–54, 63–68, 69–82
historical dimension, 17–40
historical knowledge, viii, 19, 72–74
historical method, ix, 42, 83–91, 93–102
historical study, viii, x, 17–40, 93–102, 103–23, and *passim*
history: behavioral, 22, 95–97, 99–102; Christian view of, vii, 13, 23–24, 28, 30, 35, 38, 44–46, 63–68, *passim;* critical, 88–89; definition of, 4; humanist approach to, 97–98; interpretation of, ix, 3–4, 103–23; laws in, 95; liberal view of, 6, 7, 11, 14–15, 105–8, 114–15, 120; linear, 22, 25; Marxist view of, 6, 7, 11, 14–15, 23, 42–43, 45, 48, 105–13, 116; meaning of, viii, 3–16, 44–46; narrative, ix, 84–86, 90–91; oral, 27; ordinary, 8, 12–14, 18, 48–49; patterns in, 61–68; philosophy of, ix, 44–48, 51–52, 86–87; social science, ix, 93–102; structure of, 4–11; theology of, viii; universal, 3; varieties of, viii, 17, 37, 38–39, 93, 103–4, 122; view (vision) of, 6–12, 15, 18–22, 43–44

hope, 15, 28
human nature, ix, 18, 103–4

ideology, 7, 9, 11, 105–13
Incarnation, the, 30, 87–88, 90

Jesus Christ, 12–13, 21, 24, 30, 43–44, 46
judgment, 13–14

Kuhn, Thomas, 56, 59, 75–76, 93, 110

Luther, Martin, 43, 52–53

Mandelbaum, Maurice, 81
modifications, 32–34
multifactored, ix, 7, 35–36, 103–5, 120–23
myth, 6–8

objectivism, 60
objectivity, 69–82
ontology, ix, 5–16, 20–21

Pascal, Blaise, 103–4
past-present-future, 5, 12, 25–27
periodization, periods, 3, 23, 28–29
phenomena, phenomenon, 18–21, 30–40
phases, stages, 24, 26, 34
philosophy, analytic, 44–48

process, viii–ix, 22–24, 26–27, 30, 30–38
progress, vii, 14, 23, 51
providence, viii, 11, 51

quantification, quanto-history, 93–102

reality, 18–22
Reid, Thomas, 57–59, 60
relativism, 74–75, 78
religion, 6–7, 11, 21
responsibility, human, 18, 28, 35, 38, 104

salvation, viii, 13–14, 21
Scripture, 3–16. See Bible, biblical
secular, secularist, 3, 7, 9, 19
sin, 10–11, 21, 88, 90, 103–4
social, society, 37, 105–13
spirit, spiritual, 5, 18–19, 55–68
structure, 4–12, 17–21, 39
subjectivism, 58, 59, 71–72, 74–75, 78

Tillich, Paul, 6, 8, 43
time, ix, 18, 22–30, 39, 87
Tocqueville, Alexis de, 110–12
tradition, 10, 26

vocation, 54, 86

Wolterstorff, Nicholas, 76–78